Glenna Fisy

Elsie's Paradise

The Reford Gardens

Graphic designer: Josée Amyotte
Editor: Michael Ballantyne
Copy editor: My-Trang Nguyen
Scanner operator: Mélanie Sabourin
Botanical terms: Albert Mondor

National Library of Canada cataloguing in publication

Reford, Alexander
    The Reford Gardens: Elsie's Paradise

    1. Jardins de Métis (Québec) 2. Gardens – Québec (Province).
    Grand-Métis. 3. Reford, Elsie Meighen, 1872-1967.
    4. Jardins de Métis (Québec) – Pictorial works.
    I. Tanguay, Louise. II. Title.

SB466.C33J37 2004   712'.5'09714773   C2004-940811-9

For more information about our publications,
please visit our website: www.edhomme.com
Other sites of interest: www.edjour.com • www.edtypo.com
www.edvlb.com • www.edhexagone.com

Legal deposit: second quarter 2004
Bibliothèque nationale du Québec

ISBN 2-7619-1921-1

Government of Québec – Tax credit for book publishing – Administered by
SODEC – www.sodec.gouv.qc.ca

The publisher gratefully acknowledges the support of the Société de dévelop-
pement des entreprises culturelles du Québec for its publishing program.

 Conseil des Arts   Canada Council
du Canada   for the Arts

We gratefully acknowledge the support of the Canada Council for the Arts
for its publishing program.

We acknowledge the financial support of the Government of Canada
through the Book Publishing Industry Development Program (BPIDP) for our
publishing activities.

EXCLUSIVE DISTRIBUTORS:

• For Canada
  and the United States:
  MESSAGERIES ADP*
  955 Amherst St.
  Montréal, Québec
  H2L 3K4
  Tél.: (514) 523-1182
  Fax: (514) 939-0406
  * A subsidiary of Sogides Itée

• For France and other countries:
  INTERFORUM
  Immeuble Paryseine,
  3 Allée de la Seine
  94854 Ivry Cedex
  Tél.: 01 49 59 11 89/91
  Fax: 01 49 59 11 96
  Orders: Tél.: 02 38 32 71 00
          Fax: 02 38 32 71 28

• For Switzerland:
  INTERFORUM
  P.O. Box 69 – 1701 Fribourg –
  Switzerland
  Tél.: (41-26) 460-80-60
  Fax: (41-26) 460-80-68
  Internet: www.havas.ch
  E-mail: office@havas.ch
  Distribution: OLF SA
  Z.I. 3, Corminbœuf
  P.O. Box 1061
  CH-1701 Fribourg
  Orders: Tél.: (41-26) 467-53-33
          Fax: (41-26) 467-54-66

• For Belgium and Luxembourg:
  INTERFORUM
  Boulevard de l'Europe 117
  B-1301 Wavre
  Tél.: (010) 42-03-20
  Fax: (010) 41-20-24

Elsie's Paradise

The Reford Gardens

Alexander Reford
TEXT

Louise Tanguay
PHOTOGRAPHS

LES ÉDITIONS DE
L'HOMME

Portrait of Elsie Reford at age 25, taken in 1897.

Himalayan blue poppies
(Meconopsis betonicifolia)

Acknowledgements

Writing is a solitary activity, requiring isolation and tranquillity. If I have enjoyed a little of both in recent months, it is only because I have been blessed with a team of people who have assisted me in filling the gaps I have left while absent from my duties as director of Reford Gardens.

I am grateful to several individuals who encouraged me to write this book. Questions from journalists, writers and museum consultants have pushed me to spend hours sifting through the letters, diaries and documents left by Elsie Reford. I am indebted to them for their interest. Many readers have contributed to improving the text and verifying its accuracy. They include my father, Michael Reford, and brother Lewis as well as gardeners and friends: Patricia Gallant, Helen Meredith, Mary Pratte, Mélanie Robert and Susan Woodfine. I have relied on the memoirs of my uncle, Robert Reford, and his intimate portrait of his grandmother and life at Metis. The comments of Evelyn Annett and Rachel Turgeon have been invaluable. A large team from Les Éditions de L'Homme has enthusiastically supported this project since I first broached the idea several years ago.

Two photographers have spent hours attempting to capture the essence of Elsie's garden. The first was my great-grandfather, Robert Wilson Reford. An amateur photographer from a young age, he chronicled the beauty of the garden until his death in 1951. He spent many hours in his darkroom at Grand-Metis developing and printing the images. His photographs are sometimes exquisite, sometimes ordinary. But his photographic archive is in many ways unique. He left a complete photographic record of his wife's gardens. Louise

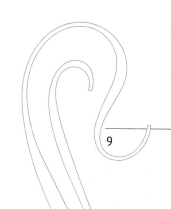

9

"The extraordinary heavy waxen texture of the petals of L. Brownii, with the very palest suspicion of Nile green shading, rich dark plum-shaded chestnut reverse and much the same colour on the anthers, together with a fragrance as illusive as it is haunting, combine to place this Lily above all praise and its success at Estevan is a source of great joy."

Elsie Reford, *Lilies at Estevan Lodge*

Elsie Reford standing near
the Mound Garden.

Tanguay has likewise walked the pathways of the gardens that Elsie Reford created. On repeated visits since the summer of 2000, in the soft light of an early July morning or the quiet blue hue of evenings in August or September, she has carefully photographed the gardens and their myriad beauties. While the worlds of these two photographers could not be more different, it is to them that we owe the record of Elsie's paradise.

Alexander Reford
Grand-Metis, March 2004

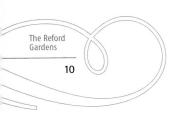

Walk flanked by dwarf
mountain pines
(*Pinus mugo*).

Preface

This book is my response to the growing interest shown in the life of my great-grand-mother, Elsie Reford, and the story of her gardens in Grand-Metis. Curiosity about her is a natural result of our efforts to promote her gardens over the past years. But her story is intriguing in its own right. The adventure of creating a garden along the St. Lawrence River appears to strike a chord with people of all ages. Over the past several years and during many talks to garden clubs in Quebec and beyond, I have sensed a growing fascination with her life and work. The audiences I have spoken to have spontaneously told me of their admiration for the woman who carved a garden out of the Quebec wilderness. And these same audiences have sometimes chastised me for not having written a book that would tell them more about her life. Gardeners are persistent folk. Their pressing demands have become a refrain too difficult to ignore.

The title of this book, *Elsie's Paradise: The Reford Gardens*, is intended to evoke the mystery of these gardens and their creator. It was very much her private paradise and one she shared with few visitors. She was in many ways a distant woman, aloof, independent and inaccessible. And while I can claim to have known her, having gone to her bedside just once or twice as a boy of four or five, I have come to know her far better through the extraordinary record she kept of her garden.

The publication of this book coincides with the opening of an exhibition dedicated to Elsie Reford at Reford Gardens. The exhibition takes its rightful place in Estevan Lodge, the fishing lodge that she made her summer home for half a century. In the room where

she once sat every evening detailing her day's work, visitors are now able to stop and read from her garden diaries and learn more about this remarkable woman. This book is a modest companion to the exhibition. As such, it is not a book solely about Elsie Reford herself or about her gardens. Nor should it be construed as the definitive word on her life. That project awaits more time and research.

Instead, *Elsie's Paradise* provides a brief glimpse of what life was like at Grand-Metis during her summers there. Although it is a complement to the exhibition, the book also stands alone. For the first time, readers will have an opportunity to hear Elsie's voice and read her own descriptions of her garden. A good deal of the text simply reproduces excerpts from her articles and diaries. I can think of no better way to do homage to her work and achievements. The selection of photographs taken during her lifetime also provides readers with an opportunity to see the gardens as she saw them.

My great-grandmother would probably be horrified to discover that her life is largely remembered today because of the gardens she created. This book will not redress the imbalance. No life can or should be reduced to a single accomplishment. In the case of Elsie Reford, who lived for 95 years, this is particularly the case. She was a woman of great range and talent. Gardening was one of her passions and one at which she excelled. But even though it consumed much of her time for more than three decades, her story is more complete and more complex. While she is widely known for the gardens she created in Grand-Metis, she would not want to be remembered for her garden alone. By reading this book you will catch glimpses of Elsie Reford – a woman like any other – with her loves and her fears, her successes and failures. You will perhaps come to the same conclusion that I have reached: that she was an extraordinary woman, both for her times and for ours.

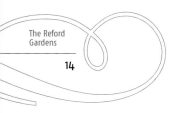

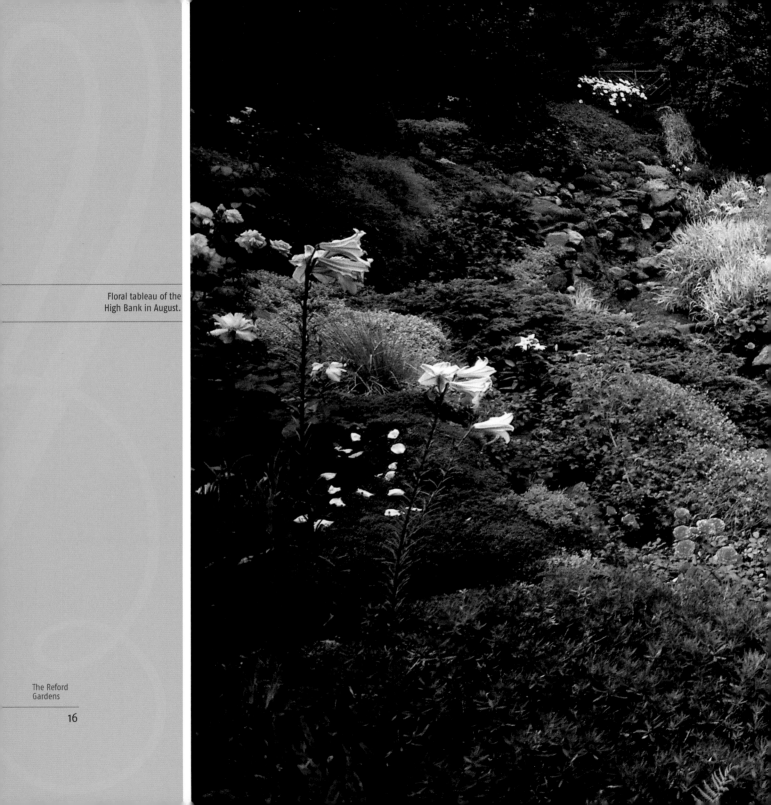

Floral tableau of the
High Bank in August.

Crab apples (*Malus* cv.) in bloom near Elsie's bench.

CHAPTER 1

"I shall always, all my life, want to come back to those sunsets."

Elsie Reford, July 20, 1913

Pages 20-21 : Crab apple trees (*Malus* cv.) in bloom in June.

Pages 22-23 : Of the several hundred portraits of Elsie Reford in her gardens, this is perhaps the best. It was taken around 1930 by her husband.

Sunset from the veranda of Estevan Lodge.

A Distant Paradise

In the summer of 1926, Elsie Reford began transforming the grounds adjacent to her fishing camp on the Mitis River into a garden. A few degrees south of the 49th parallel, the gardens she created over the next 30 years were the northernmost in eastern Canada. Known to some as Les Jardins de Métis, to others as Reford Gardens, they have become renowned since opening to the public in 1962.

Elsie Reford's is a garden of character. It is bold and unique, innovative but traditional. Few gardens have been built under such difficult conditions. Hundreds of miles from the nearest plant nursery, Elsie Reford faced countless challenges when she set herself this formidable task. She took a spruce forest and shaped it into a garden that boasted one of the largest collections of plants in its day. She excavated and dug, built stone walls and moved trees. She brought boulders from neighbouring fields and placed them one by one in the garden. She created fine compost required for exotic plants with leaves she had bartered from local farmers. Where experienced plantsmen had failed, she succeeded in transplanting or propagating rare species, like azaleas and blue poppies, and adapting them to the Quebec climate. She trained local men, farmers and fishing guides, making them expert gardeners. Together, they built a remarkable garden over three decades. With the help of her husband, Robert Wilson Reford, an amateur photographer, she chronicled the genesis and development of the garden with scientific precision.

Waterfalls on the Mitis River, circa 1920.

Mouth of the Mitis River below Estevan Lodge, circa 1900.

Elsie Reford was born Elsie Stephen Meighen on January 22, 1872. She grew up in Montreal and was educated there and in Paris and Dresden, Germany. Her father, Robert Meighen, was president of the Lake of the Woods Milling Company, makers of Five Roses flour and the largest flour milling company in the British Empire. Her mother, Elsie Stephen, was the youngest sister of George Stephen, who had made a fortune building and operating a railway from St. Paul, Minnesota, into Manitoba in the 1870s. The St. Paul, Minneapolis and Manitoba Railway was the foundation of a business empire that spanned the North American continent and made Stephen and his principal partners, his cousin Donald Smith (later Lord Strathcona) and J.J. Hill, three of the wealthiest men of their time. In 1880, Stephen founded the Canadian Pacific Railway. As its president and principal financier, he was chiefly responsible for building the transcontinental railway that linked Montreal to Vancouver. Stephen's accomplishment and contribution to the unity of the British Empire earned him recognition from Queen Victoria. Shortly after the completion of the railway in November 1885, he was made a baronet and became known as "Sir George Stephen, baronet, of Montreal and Grand-Metis, Quebec."

Stephen lived in Montreal, but took several weeks off every summer to fish for salmon on the rivers of eastern Quebec. He bought 100 acres of property overlooking the Mitis River in 1886. In 1887, he built Estevan Lodge, a rambling wooden building sufficiently large to accommodate his fishing parties. Estevan Lodge is built on a promontory above the confluence of the Mitis and St. Lawrence rivers. The site was described in 1815 by the surveyor and mapmaker Joseph Bouchette:

"The grand river Mitis discharges itself 24 miles below Rimouski into Anse aux Snelles, an expansive estuary, which is easily forded at low water. Mr. Larrivé's dwelling-house and establishment stand at the mouth of the river, across which booms are

This photograph shows Estevan Lodge much like it was when first built in 1887.

Portrait of George Stephen, 1897.

extended to retain the deals turned off from the saw-mill, situated about two miles and a half higher up, occupying a most advantageous site. At the foot of the falls that are used in working the mill, the river forms an almost circular basin, bounded by a perpendicular rock of about 200 feet, excepting to the eastward, where the ground is woody but of equal elevation. The mill itself is awfully situated on the deep inclination of the falls, and the uproar of the machinery, the loudness and beauty of the cascade, combine with the peculiar wildness of the scenery, to render the spot extremely romantic. The proprietor of this mill is generally a large timber contractor; and vessels usually receive their cargoes at Mitis, where they may lie at anchor off Anse aux Snelles – somewhat exposed, however, to the forces of the tides and stress of weather." (*Topographical Dictionary of Lower Canada*)

The mouth of the river was an active port for most of the nineteenth century. The village of Grand-Metis developed nearby, with a post office, blacksmith's forge, and the offices of Price Brothers, who owned the timber limits along the Mitis River to the south. The promontory upon which Estevan Lodge was built was uninhabited and undeveloped.

George Stephen purchased the property in two stages. On July 14, 1886 he obtained the eastern side of the Mitis River from Archibald Ferguson, a local landowner. Ferguson had acquired the vestiges of the De Peiras *seigneurie* from the McNider family, who had in turn bought it from the descendants of the original seigneur. The 40-acre property was bordered to the north by the St. Lawrence, south by the road along the edge of the river, west by the Price Brothers property along the Mitis River, and east by the farm of W.E. Page. It was on this piece of land that Stephen would build his fishing camp. The west side of the Mitis River and the Pointe aux Cenelles (a *cenelle* or *snelle* is the berry of the hawthorn) Stephen acquired from Ulric-Joseph Tessier, a judge from nearby Rimouski.

The old wooden bridge over the Mitis River was replaced
by the present bridge in 1929.

George Stephen's fishing camp, "Les Fourches," on the Matapedia River at Causapscal, circa 1880.

Lady Mount Stephen with fishing guides Douglas Berchervaise and Lewis Eden, 33-lb salmon, length 40 inches, caught in Sir Donald's Pool, July 24, 1923.

This became a farm that supplied Estevan with fresh produce, milk and butter. Stephen bought a strip of land along the river from its mouth to the falls, four miles to the south. By accumulating the lots and land along the river, he ensured that he alone had the right to fish. Over time, and with the expenditure of large sums of money, Stephen finally acquired what he was convinced would be an idyllic place to practise fly-fishing for salmon.

Sufficiently enthused by the possibilities of the Mitis River, Stephen decided to abandon his fishing camp at the forks of the Causapscal and Matapedia rivers, 100 miles to the south. Quite what led Stephen to forsake his camp, "Les Fourches," at Causapscal is unknown. Perhaps because it was so close to the busy tracks of the Intercolonial Railway. Perhaps he sought more peaceful waters or spacious quarters. Or it may have been that, like others, he wished to exchange the sultry summer days common in the valley of the Matapedia River for the cool night air along the St. Lawrence. Whatever the reasons, Stephen gave away several hundred acres to his former employees and sold some of the best salmon pools in the world to the Restigouche Fishing Club.

The waters on the Mitis River were comparatively unknown and untried. They had rarely been fished because the river was the site of timber operations which made fishing hazardous, if not impossible. Mud and stick dams had been built across the river by the lumber companies in several areas in order to contain the logs floated downriver. Stephen was not alone in seeing the river's potential. In 1860, an English angler and author, Colonel Sir James Edward Alexander, hinted at the potential of the Mitis River:

"...in spite of spears and saw-logs they managed to hook and lose and kill a few large salmon...if an angler happened to be at Metis at the proper season – June –

Lord Bessborough, the Governor-General of Canada, being guided on the Mitis River, 1935.

Guests fishing on the Mitis River.

he would stand a good chance of killing some large fish, and of losing a great many also; and that if the *Seigneur* keeps his word, removes the dam, and clears the river of logs, it may prove to be worth some thousands a year to him as a salmon river." (*Salmon Fishing In Canada*)

Estevan Lodge was the name George Stephen gave to his fishing camp on its completion in 1887. The name comes from the cable code that Stephen used for his confidential correspondence. During the 1880s when he was frantically knitting together the financing to build the CPR, Stephen would receive hundreds of coded telegrams addressed to "Estevan," his confidential cipher. Some think the word is a conflation of Stephen and Van Horne, the surname of the general manager of the CPR, William Van Horne, who was the author of many of the urgent messages. But it could also be a variant on Esteban, the Spanish equivalent of Stephen. Whatever its origins, Estevan was the name the building and property had for most of its history. After the building was opened to the public in 1962, the lodge was rebaptized the "Villa Reford" to pay homage to Elsie Reford and her family. More recently, in honour of the reopening of the building after its restoration in 2003, it was again renamed and is now referred to as *Estevan Lodge* in English and the *Villa Estevan* in French.

There is perhaps a deliberate irony in Stephen giving his peaceful retreat the name that symbolized the most frantic period of his life. Estevan was intended to be a harbour of quietude and an oasis of peace. Stephen fished with his wife and their friends on the Mitis River, quietly casting in the fast-flowing waters. Even though he entertained his business partners and political allies at Estevan, his real interest was in fishing rather than finance.

A Distant Paradise

Visits to the gardens are punctuated by five bridges that traverse the stream.

This early watercolour of Estevan shows the rustic simplicity of the lodge and its rudimentary landscaping.

Every surface inside Estevan, such as this table in Elsie's sitting room, was decorated with fresh flowers.

The property was extensive but only modestly landscaped. It was described in this way in 1894:

"The house is reached by an avenue of 1500 feet in length and 24 in width, constructed of broken stone and gravel and properly graded. The grounds are well wooded and in excellent order, and, being high above the bay, command a fine view of the Gulf of the St. Lawrence. There are also suitable facilities for sea bathing. Separated from the grounds by a grove of trees are the house of the caretaker, stables, coach house, barns, etc. all new and well kept, and adjoining this a large area of pasture land. The whole is surrounded by a well constructed paling fence with substantial gates...there is no more picturesque or healthful spot on the Lower St. Lawrence."

Estevan Lodge was built in the summer of 1887. The identity of the architect is unknown, although it is possible that Stephen used the services of William Tutin Thomas, the man who had designed his Montreal mansion several years earlier. Records show that the architect of Estevan was paid $180. The original structure was simpler than the building we know today. It had only one storey. The house was clad in clapboard painted white and had a cedar shingle roof stained an oxblood colour. The bedrooms were arranged along a long, narrow corridor. From the sitting room and dining room the views over the Mitis River and towards Mont-Comi were splendid. They were unimpeded by the trees that today obscure the river from view. The veranda, which envelops Estevan Lodge on three sides, is in many ways the most attractive room in the house. There, with his wife and fishing friends, Stephen would sit in the evenings after a long day on the river, bathed in the pink hues of the sunsets, perhaps sipping a dram imported from one of the Speyside distilleries near his birthplace in Dufftown, Scotland. Estevan Lodge was also

The driveway to Estevan Lodge, around 1904.

Following pages: View to the north towards Pointe-aux-Cenelles and the island in the bay of the Mitis River.

sited to take advantage of the beauty of the sunsets. When the sun falls below the horizon during the summer solstice, it sets square in the centre of the ornate columns that support the veranda.

The original Estevan had 13 rooms. A substantial pantry connected the building to the service wing, which had a large kitchen. The servants' quarters were also at the rear of the building. There, some of the kitchen and domestic staff were housed during the summer months. Adjacent to Estevan was an icehouse, where the salmon were stored on blocks of ice cut in the deep winter from the Mitis River and enveloped in sawdust to slow their melting. A water tower topped with a windmill pumped fresh water from the stream into a cistern, thereby providing the house with water for cooking and bathing. Estevan Lodge was a poor cousin of Stephen's Montreal home. Only the high ceilings and ornate hardware show an architectural parentage with his Drummond Street residence, an Italianate *palazzo* of stone and exotic woodwork. Estevan is indeed a rather clumsy architectural ensemble. But it was practical and welcoming. And the fishing was what was important.

The interior panelling of Estevan Lodge is of Douglas fir, often called British Columbia fir. At the time that Estevan was built, B.C. fir was only just beginning to be exported to eastern Canada from the west-coast forests. The completion of the CPR in 1885 and the inauguration of a regular transcontinental train service in 1886 made the wood more readily available for construction. B.C. fir is costly today, but at the time it was among the least expensive woods. Stephen appears to have become enchanted by its qualities when he made his first inspection tour of the CPR lines in 1886 and ordered some for Estevan. The shipment of B.C. fir destined to be used at Grand-Metis was reportedly one of the first consignments to traverse Canada on the newly completed railway.

A Distant
Paradise

Estevan Lodge was sparsely furnished in comparison to Stephen's Drummond Street mansion. Stephen was evidently seeking a simpler life when he fished. The furniture was fairly unostentatious, with only discreet ornamentation. Made by a Montreal furniture maker, S.R. Parsons, it cost Stephen $3,712. Most of it was dispersed when Estevan Lodge was sold to the government of Quebec in 1961. The furniture for Estevan is quite recognizable. We have been able to recover several pieces because of the distinctive style of the cabinetry and the maker's stamp on the underside of each piece. In spite of its relative simplicity, Estevan was a significant investment. Stephen's accountant estimated the cost of building Estevan Lodge to have been $38,000 and the total cost of the estate, including the lodge, the land and the landscaping to be $73,426.

Even after taking up permanent residence in London in 1891, Stephen returned to fish at Grand-Metis in the summer. But his dream of a fishing camp where he and his wife would fish together came to an end in April 1896 when she died in their London home. He never again returned to Estevan. "I couldn't," he told his friend Garnet Wolseley, "I was never on that river without her, and I should be reminded of her every moment." Stephen contemplated selling Estevan and drew up a detailed description of the property to entice his friend and partner, J.J. Hill. But Hill, who made the trek from St. Paul, Minnesota, to his own fishing camp on the north shore of the St. Lawrence, preferred to stay put on the Rivière St. Jean.

From the 1890s onwards, Estevan Lodge welcomed Stephen's friends and associates. They included sportsmen like Percy Rockefeller and business magnates such as James Stillman, president of the National City Bank of New York (better known today as Citi-corp). Gaspard Farrer, his friend and financial advisor at Barings, a London investment bank, made the journey from England to Grand-Metis every summer to try his luck on

the river. But the most regular visitors were Elsie Reford and John W. Sterling. Elsie and her family enjoyed use of the river in August and Sterling had it for July.

John Sterling had the run of Estevan because he had long served as one of Stephen's closest advisors. Founder of an important Wall Street law firm, Shearman and Sterling, he was the lawyer for the New York agency of the Bank of Montreal and managed Stephen's and Donald Smith's legal affairs. A partner in several of their railway endeavours, he became one of the richest men in the United States, leaving more than $29 million to his *alma mater*, Yale University. He was also eccentric. A fastidious bachelor, he would sometimes shut himself inside Estevan for days on end. Sterling's death at Grand-Metis, in what the *New York Times* dubbed "Lord Mount Stephen's castle," freed Stephen to fulfil a promise he had made many years earlier. He made a gift of Estevan Lodge to Elsie Reford on September 12, 1918. Three years later, he died at his English country house, Brocket Hall, aged 92.

Exactly why Stephen chose Elsie as the recipient of Estevan is unknown. Reportedly Stephen's favourite niece, she shared his love of salmon fishing. Every season, she would write her uncle detailing the size of the fish she had caught and the pools where she had had the greatest success. She was also the daughter of his favourite sister, and appears to have nurtured a deep admiration for her uncle. A keen judge of human nature, Stephen recognized the talents and intelligence of his niece. When she lived in England for extended periods during the First World War, she saw him regularly, visiting Brocket and enjoying his company and that of his second wife, Gian. Stephen had no children of his own, but had an adopted daughter named Alice. He had already given her a house in London and her husband, Lord Northcote, the Governor-General of Australia from 1904 to 1908, had provided her with financial security. As Elsie had inherited

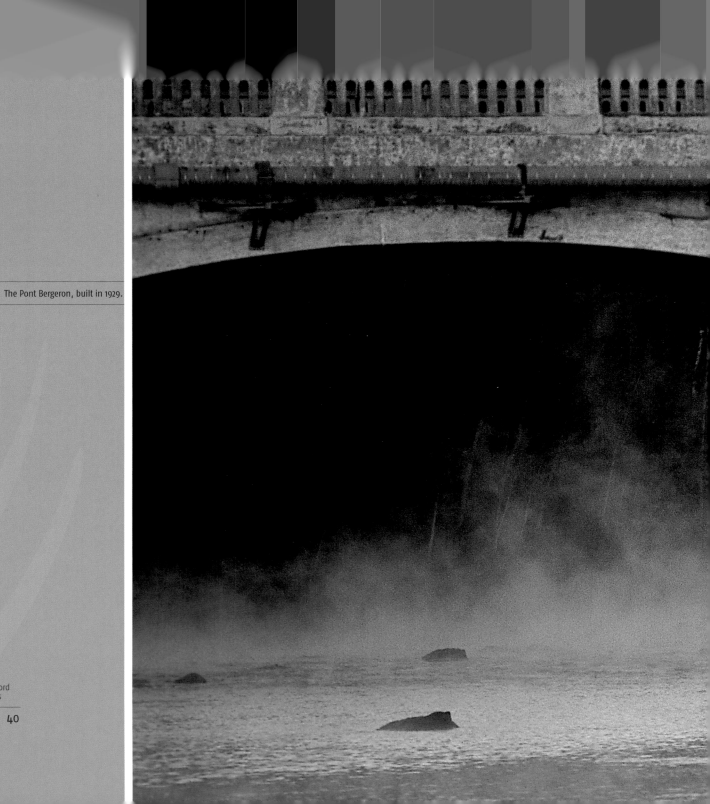

The Pont Bergeron, built in 1929.

View looking north from
the balcony of Estevan Lodge.

Elsie is wearing a silk *ceinture fléchée*
around her waist, which she kept
at a svelte 17 inches throughout
most of her life.

a third of her father's fortune after his death in 1911, she also had a private income to maintain the guardians and guides on the river as well as the large staff who worked at Estevan Lodge. And in her husband, Robert Wilson Reford, she had a companion who shared her love of the region and the outdoors, and who loved Estevan almost as much as his wife.

The legacy Stephen left to Elsie Reford was not limited to the property. It included as well the high esteem which he had cultivated in the region. The *curé* of the parish of St. Octave, Louis–Jacques Langis, wrote her in 1909, "you represent, here, a man for whose memory I have a great respect and admiration. I had not the honour to know Lord Mount Stephen personally, but I heard how liberal, generous he has been and is still towards French Canadians; there is no bigotry in him and I know he has been a sincere friend to French Canadians. What I admire in the Uncle, I admire in the niece."

Elsie Reford practised the violin daily until her duties as a volunteer during World War I led her to abandon her musical ritual.

Elsie Reford's Violin

Music was part of every young woman's education in bourgeois Montreal. Elsie, her sister Margaret, and her brother Frank Meighen were all schooled in music. Elsie played both the violin and the piano. Frank took his love of music to such lengths that he personally bankrolled the Montreal Opera Company to the tune of more than $100,000 in losses over three years, from 1910–1913. Margaret also loved music – but she loved the music master more. She ran off and married him, causing endless grief for her parents and contributing to a turbulent life.

Elsie's violin was an early nineteenth-century instrument made by the Klotz family of Mittenwald, Germany, violin makers since the seventeenth century. Her bow was manufactured by a famous Parisian bow and violin maker, Collin-Mezin. But the case is almost as beautiful to the eye. A gift from her father, it was made in London by E. Withers and Co. An embroidered cover, with her initials (ESM for Elsie Stephen Meighen), accompanied the instrument. She played the violin every day for many years, only stopping when her commitments during the First World War made it impossible to continue. Years later, when she was largely confined to her bed, her grandchildren got together to buy her an audio system. In her 90s, she began listening to records, rekindling memories of her musical youth.

Following pages: One of the early flowering peonies from Elsie's collection, the rare *Paeonia veitchii*.

CHAPTER 2

"Here of a summer's night, when there is one of those rare all-pervading stillnesses and the world seems wrapped in a sacred silence, broken only by the slow rhythm of the sea lapping its waters upon the shore; with the moon, silver clear in a cloudless sky, flood-lighting every petal of every lily and the upturned face of every flower, the ineffable beauty of the scene transcends time and place to bring an awareness of the eternal beyond and of a closeness to it."

Elsie Reford, *A Lily Garden in the Lower St. Lawrence Valley*

Pages 48-49: The High Bank in its August glory.

Pages 50-51: The High Bank 60 years earlier.

Turkscap lily
(*Lilium martagon*).

An Adventure in Gardening

Gardening was by no means Elsie Reford's first calling. From the early 1900s she had come to Grand-Metis to fish the pools on the river. She also rode, canoed and hunted. She fished every summer without fail. Then in 1926 she suffered an attack of appendicitis. Surgery ensued and her doctors ordered her to convalesce. Relaxation, reading, and certainly no fishing, was the regime. Perhaps a little gardening would do to pass the time. Elsie Reford was 54 years old.

During the summer of 1926, she began laying out the gardens and supervising their construction. The gardens took 10 years to build, extending over more than 20 acres. When she began, with the exception of a flagpole, a cedar hedge and a tree-lined driveway, the property was barely landscaped at all. The grass was cut to feed the horses. Flowerpots were arranged on the veranda. It was, after all, a fishing lodge.

Although she had shown no predilection for gardening as a young woman, her interest was deeply rooted. Her uncle's Montreal mansion had an extensive orchard and garden as well as a conservatory for ferns and tropical plants. After her father bought the house in 1900, his orchid collection was thrown open for public visits organized by the Montreal Horticultural Society. Prior to the First World War, she became interested in the Garden City movement, a loosely knit coalition of architects, landscape architects, planners and philanthropists who sought to improve housing for industrial workers and create

Elsie Reford during a visit to Brocket Hall, her uncle's country house in Hertfordshire, England.

A garden is never finished – Elsie Reford at work in the gardens.

Elsie Reford admiring one of her favourite plants, the white turkscap lily (*Lilium martagon* var. *album*).

better living conditions in cities. Elsie Reford promoted the creation of a garden suburb in Montreal and was active on several committees that sought to improve the quality of school playgrounds throughout the city.

Like many garden builders in North America, she drew inspiration from her frequent visits to English gardens and to the parks and grounds of English country houses. As the Canadian director of the Cunard Line, whose passenger ships travelled from Montreal to Southampton and Liverpool, Robert Wilson Reford attended annual board meetings in England. Elsie Reford usually accompanied him and took advantage of their time in England to visit gardens. She was also a frequent guest at her uncle's country house, Brocket Hall, which sat among extensive grounds and gardens.

With only occasional references to guide us, it is difficult to establish the extent to which the gardens she saw and the gardeners she met in England influenced her personal interest in gardening. Whatever the provenance of her passion, Elsie Reford's gardens were very much her own creation. She deliberately refrained from seeking professional help. "There has been no landscape architect to head off mistakes, costly in time and work to remedy but each one of them teaching something," she wrote in 1949. Perhaps as a result, her gardens are remarkably free of formality and ornamentation, and show few obvious quotations from other gardens. Rather than create a series of garden rooms adjacent to the house, she chose instead to develop what is really a series of gardens. They are nestled alongside the banks of Page's Brook, a stream that threads its way through the property.

"Nowhere is there any formal planting," she wrote, "there are no flower beds, the gardens having been fashioned more or less to follow the twisting and curving of the little stream with short stretches of woods left here and there between them." The result

This panoramic photograph captures the tamed wildness of the gardens.

Stepping stones allowed Elsie and her gardeners to traverse the brook.

is strikingly original. Elsie Reford designed a path that meanders from one garden to another, occasionally interrupted by bridges spanning the brook.

Elsie Reford had to overcome many difficulties as she worked to bring her garden to life. First among them were the allergies that sometimes left her bedridden for days on end. This was finally cured by repeated visits to her doctors. The second obstacle was the property itself. Estevan was first and foremost a fishing lodge. The site was chosen because of its proximity to a salmon river and its dramatic views − not for the quality of the soil. And so, when she began digging, she quickly realized how forbidding the task of building a garden at Grand-Metis would be. "In the matter of good natural soil Estevan has been rather niggardly dealt with," she wrote. "When the first gardens came to be carved out it was found that there was nothing adequate for horticultural purposes."

The topsoil was poor and underneath there was nothing but clay. To counteract nature's deficiencies, she created soil for each of the plants she had selected, bringing peat and sand from her farms. "Time and patience were largely drawn upon to transfer and mix thoroughly these two ingredients and bring up gravel from the beaches to add to them. Leaf mould presented more of a difficulty, for there were not sufficient deciduous trees in our woods to supply all that has been required, but that too has been overcome by resorting to a system of barter − salmon from the Mitis River being exchanged for leaves from a neighbour's grove." This exchange must have appeared fortuitous to the local farmers who were then suffering through the Great Depression. Then, as now, the gardens provided much-needed work for an area with chronically high unemployment.

Elsie Reford's genius as a gardener was born of the knowledge she developed regarding the needs of each plant. Over the course of her long life, she became an expert plantsman.

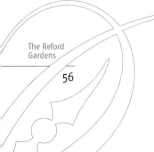

Following pages: The High Bank.

She detailed her work in garden diaries which she kept religiously each day of every summer. Her entries were often mundane, but they are invaluable today as work proceeds to restore the gardens she created. By the end of her life, Elsie Reford was able to counsel other gardeners, writing articles in the journals of the Royal Horticultural Society and the North American Lily Society about her success in growing plants in a cold climate. She was humble about her expertise, but visitors marvelled at her encyclopaedic knowledge.

When she began, there were few examples for her to follow. The province of Quebec has boasted gardens since the first colonists arrived in the sixteenth century, but no one had tried gardening in the Lower St. Lawrence region, and certainly not on the scale that Elsie Reford envisioned. "The gardens," she wrote, "are geographically placed where a climate of forbidding severity might well be expected." To her surprise, she found the property ideal for the cultivation of exotic perennials. Its proximity to the St. Lawrence and Mitis rivers provides generous levels of atmospheric moisture. In winter, the average snowfall of 11½ feet or more over the course of the winter offers a fleecy blanket that protects the gardens. The snow arrives early (in November) and leaves late (in May), insulating plants from the harsh winter winds, killer frosts, and the severe temperatures that can range as low as − 35°C in January and February. Although the region is considered as part of Hardiness Zone 4, plants judged hardy to Zone 6 often endure the climate and sometimes thrive. While days without frost are few (110 on average), the short season has the effect of encouraging rapid growth. Plants burst into life once the snow melts. The long days and additional hours of sunlight in midsummer help in the plants' growth cycle. In summer, the daytime and nighttime temperatures vary considerably, with warm days and cool nights. The cool night air helps to maintain bloom, which can endure longer than in other gardens. These conditions proved to be ideal for such plants

"In the matter of good natural soil Estevan has been rather niggardly dealt with. When the first gardens came to be carved out it was found that there was nothing adequate for horticultural purposes. However, most fortunately, there were unlimited quantities of rich peaty soil and good sand in the fields nearby. Eighteen years ago, when the gardens were begun, it was before the days of labour difficulties and excessively high wages, so these could be brought by horse and cart to wherever they were required. Three foot trenches were laboriously dug, six inches of manure placed in the bottom and then a mixture of three parts peat soil to one of sand with generous supply of equal parts of sheep manure and bone meal thoroughly sifted and mixed, put in and firmly packed down. As time went on a compost heap came into being and the peat was reduced by one part and replaced with compost. Except when preparing ground for roses and azaleas, whole requirements must be respected, this formula has been followed throughout; but for the last four or five years wherever a lily bulb has been planted, it has been embedded in about three inches of very finely ground rotted leaves with some wood ash and bone meal."

Elsie Reford, *A Lily Garden in the Lower St. Lawrence Valley*

Spruce trees provide the gardens with their form and intimacy, an evergreen backdrop to Elsie's collection of perennials.

as the Tibetan blue poppy and the alpines, providing an environment similar to that which they enjoy in their native habitat.

Elsie Reford gradually discovered that several microclimates existed within the garden itself. The most fragile plants, such as azaleas or blue poppies, not generally hardy to such climes, were placed in protected pockets, where they did not suffer the ill effects of biting winds. She knew she was being adventurous. Her excitement is hinted at in her garden diary for May 25, 1939: "...tried planting as a great innovation a shrub, namely an *Acer palmatum atropurpureum*... It is an experiment and may succeed." She was likely one of the first gardeners in Quebec to try the Japanese red maple. The effort was rewarded. Photographs from the 1950s show more than 30 growing in what must have been the most severe climate they had yet experienced in North America.

Elsie Reford had no training of any kind as a garden designer. While she collected and appreciated art, she laid no claim to artistic talent. Her approach to garden design was thus largely intuitive, guided more by the topography of the site than any desire to impose a design upon the landscape. She also read widely. In addition to the standard works on plants, we know that her library contained several books by the influential English garden designer and writer Gertrude Jekyll, and a well-thumbed copy of *The English Flower Garden* by William Robinson, who pioneered "wild gardening" and the use of indigenous plants and natural plantings. From her reading and her own appreciation of the landscape, Elsie Reford designed a garden that integrates native and exotic plants in a flowing, naturalistic fashion.

There is only one straight line in the gardens. "There is perhaps a very slight approach to something of a formal nature," she wrote, "in the double herbaceous border of over

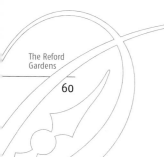

The Reford
Gardens

60

300 feet in length, hence its name 'The Long Walk.' From its 7-foot path, between the sloping borders each 12 feet wide, there is a vista across to the far blue hills of the north shore." It is here that we find Elsie Reford at her most flamboyant. The Long Walk is in bloom from the moment the snow melts until the first frost, with a careful selection of plants providing a succession of bloom. Lilacs are succeeded by peonies, delphiniums, lilies and roses, a progression of bloom and fragrance, supplemented by a judicious selection of perennials and the occasional annual. The quantities were prodigious.

Each garden had its particularities and over time, each was given a name. By naming a garden, Elsie bestowed on it both a personality and a permanence. During a visit in the 1930s, she named a garden in honour of her eldest grandson, Robert; it was thereafter known as "Robert's Garden." Not surprisingly, her other grandchildren wanted their own gardens, too. Another grandson laid claim to the scree. She agreed only reluctantly, not certain that the garden would prove to be a success. When it did, she sometimes referred to it as "Michael's miracle." So it was that my father was given his own garden. Over the years her remaining grandchildren, Maryon, Boris, Sonja and Alexis all had gardens named in their honour.

Elsie Reford's gardens were intended strictly for her personal enjoyment. They were opened to the public on rare occasions. While she did not actively shun visitors, she did not encourage them either. On occasion, botanists and gardeners would pay a visit. Among them was Henry Teuscher, conservator of the Montreal Botanical Garden. Trained in Berlin, Teuscher designed the municipal garden and oversaw its construction from 1936 to 1938. He paid several visits to Elsie Reford's gardens during the 1940s, and became convinced of their importance. Later, in 1960, when Elsie Reford's son, Brigadier Bruce Reford, began to question his own ability to maintain the gardens his mother had

Elsie leaving The Long Walk.

Regal lilies *(Lilium regale)* on The Long Walk.

"It had better be explained that nowhere in the Estevan gardens are Lilies growing in beds, or in anything approaching one. They are always in combination with other plants; in herbaceous borders, among shrubs of all kinds, among species and hybrid Roses, in unorthodox rock gardens and indeed everywhere where there is cultivated ground and nowhere where the slightest aspersions could be cast upon the drainage, for this, in experience here, is the chief concern of Lilies."

Elsie Reford, *Lilies at Estevan Lodge*

Birdbaths occasionally provide a resting-place for a fallen beauty.

Page's Brook offers a musical accompaniment to the gardens.

The High Bank was traversed by steps and pathways, facilitating access to the gardens.

Architect Jennifer Luce created a garden, *Transfusion*, for the International Garden Festival that paid homage to Elsie Reford and her passion both for fishing and gardening.

left him, Teuscher intervened, offering to lobby the government of Quebec. He hoped the government would transform the gardens into a centre for research into Nordic plants. While the research station was never created, Teuscher's arguments did prevail, and the government acquired the gardens in 1961, spotting an opportunity to develop tourism in eastern Quebec. The gardens were opened to the public the following year and their popularity has grown ever since. The government played an important, indeed crucial, role in preserving the gardens. Fortunately, successive managers of the gardens have seen their role as essentially custodial, maintaining the gardens rather than transforming them.

Since 1995, the gardens have been owned by Les Amis des Jardins de Métis, a charitable organization created to ensure their preservation and development. With the help of a team of horticulturists and gardeners, board members and friends of the gardens, the organization has undertaken a complete restoration of the site. Elsie Reford's gardens have become more widely appreciated through articles in magazines and television documentaries. Since the summer of 2000, the gardens have hosted the International Garden Festival. This has quickly become one of the leading contemporary garden design events in the world. More than 100 designers, architects, landscape architects and garden designers have contributed to the festival since that time. Their work has challenged the very notion of the garden and their creations have been both provocative and amusing. While they have pushed the idea of the garden in directions Elsie Reford would neither have understood nor approved, the festival's designers have continued the adventure she initiated at Grand-Metis in the 1920s.

Treading the ground one's ancestors walked is an emotional experience. But when that ground has also been shaped, planted and cultivated by a woman as extraordinary as

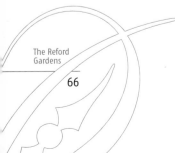

"A more perfect *[day]* *[could]* not be imagined.
Spent some *[time]* *[in e]*ach of the gardens and
each held the*[ir own]* beauty of spring with
views and vis*[tas]* *[enc]*hanting wherever one
looked. *[Wh]*at *[lov]*liness comes out of
moth*[er ea]*rth if one *[ta]*kes care of her."

26 mai 1937

"On ne pourrait imaginer une journée plus
parfaite. J'ai passé un peu de temps dans
chacun des jardins et tous présentaient une
beauté printanière particulière, avec des
ouvertures et des vues enchanteresses
partout où le regard portait. Quels charmes
émanent de Mère nature quand on s'occupe
d'elle."

The Living Room, Bernard Saint-Denis and Peter Fianu's remarkable garden for the 2000 edition of the International Garden Festival.

Quebec landscape architects NIP Paysage created this thought-provoking garden, intended to illustrate the transformation of the landscape by modern forestry and the genetic manipulation of plants.

Claude Cormier's *Blue Stick Garden* has become an icon of contemporary garden design since it was first exhibited at the International Garden Festival in 2000.

The pond is a quiet refuge, favoured by birds and popular with visitors.

Robert Wilson Reford was both a painter and a photographer and used to sketch on the banks of the Mitis River.

Opposite page: Robert Reford's Kodak panoramic camera.

Elsie Reford, this emotional attachment also becomes a responsibility. In Elsie's case, the preservation of her legacy is assisted by the careful records she kept of her gardens. Every day of every week of every summer, she carefully noted her work in the gardens. Robert Wilson Reford chronicled the evolution of the gardens with a photographer's eye and the dogged regularity of a dutiful husband. This dual record, of documents and photographs, is perhaps unique in the annals of gardening. They are precious records that permit us to understand the evolution of the gardens and guide our actions in developing them.

Preserving an historic garden is fraught with challenges. In our case, we have been slowly removing the accretions which have hidden the gardens' treasures, replacing furniture and fencing, and restoring some of the lost plant collections. Elsie Reford's diaries have encouraged us in our efforts to reintroduce the plants that inspired her, chosen because of their delicate palette, their fragrance, or the challenge of growing them in the northern environment of Grand-Metis.

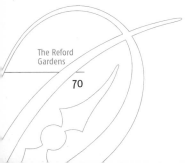

Panoramic Camera

Robert Wilson Reford is credited with being Canada's first amateur photographer. In 1888, Eastman Kodak introduced the Kodak No. 1 box camera, and one of the first to buy the new apparatus was Robert Wilson Reford. Aged 21, he had recently returned from France and Belgium where his father had sent him to learn French and serve as an apprentice in a shipping company. In 1889, he travelled across Canada with his camera, snapping photographs of muddy Winnipeg, the soaring peaks of Alberta and the recently constructed train trestles in the canyons of British Columbia.

His purchase was not greeted with much enthusiasm by his stern father. Writing from his office in Montreal, Robert Reford Senior chastised his son for buying the Kodak and more particularly for having bought it on credit – leaving him to foot the bill.

The Kodak camera cost $25 and came loaded with film for 100 exposures. It introduced an entirely new method of photography – point and shoot – and made photography accessible to a much broader public – travellers and tourists in particular – requiring little or no technical experience. When the photos were taken and the film used up, the camera was sent to George Eastman's Kodak laboratories in Rochester, New York. It was returned with the photographs and loaded with film for another 100 photos. Kodak's slogan was "You press the button. We do the rest."

When he arrived in Victoria, Robert Wilson Reford began to take pictures of what was then a frontier town, a settlement of muddy streets, mills and wharves, very different from the pristine city we know today. His most interesting photographs are of Vancouver Island's two minorities – the Chinese and the indigenous peoples. His father's Mount Royal Rice Milling and Manufacturing Company in Victoria employed many Chinese, who were among the company's clients. Robert Reford's photographs show his subjects in casual poses, illustrative of how the Kodak camera allowed photographers to capture people in more candid mode than was often possible for professionals with their cumbersome glass-plate equipment.

As ship agent on the Mount Royal Rice Mill's transport vessel – the famous clipper ship, the *Thermopylae* – Robert Reford travelled up and down the coast of British Columbia. In 1890, while on a trip along the northwest coast of Vancouver Island and the Queen Charlotte Islands, he photographed Haida villages and their inhabitants. His photographs captured the majesty and sadness of the villages at Masset, Port Simpson, Port Essington and Metlakatla. Unlike the other photographers who had visited these communities, he was less interested in the Haida totems and more concerned with the Haida themselves. His photographs of the Haida chief and pioneer native artist, Albert Edward Edenshaw, are among the most evocative.

Robert Reford used two darkrooms, one of which was built under the eaves after the family enlarged Estevan in 1926. From his very first visits to Metis, he took photographs of his wife's property. So began a love affair with Estevan, whose evolution he chronicled for almost 50 years.

Elsie Reford and friend, circa 1958.

Elsie's palette: shrub roses *(Rosa rugosa)* accompanied by penstemon *(Pentstemon jamesii)*.

Pages 74-75 : A new planting of wildflowers on the site of the International Garden Festival.

"It is just after 8 o'clock and I am sitting in front of my big window with the gorgeous panorama of a glorious afterglow from a perfect sunset. There is every hue of blue on the waters of 'the Blue Lagoon' while Pointe-aux-Cenelles is bathed in pinks and crimson and the dark hills of the north shore seem no further than two or three miles distant. I don't think in the whole world at this moment there could be anything more beautiful."

Elsie Reford, June 2, 1931

Pages 76-77 : Page's Brook with yellow loosestrife *(lysimachia punctata)* in bloom.

Pages 78-79 : A view of the mouth of the Mitis River in 1902.

The sunsets from Estevan Lodge are often breathtaking.

A Day in Paradise

Life for Elsie Reford was a series of rituals. Order and organization were principles that governed her decisions and guided her actions. While different rituals applied in the city and the country, the routine at Grand-Metis was a mirror of the life led in Montreal.

The day was arranged around Elsie Reford. She was not only the principal occupant of Estevan, she was also the owner of the property. As such, the household revolved around her, rather than her husband. Each day began in the same way. Her lady's maid would bring morning tea to her room and open the curtains. Rising late, Elsie Reford would not appear downstairs until past 9:30 a.m., after breakfast had been served to the guests and family. She would exchange greetings with the butler, Mr. Bufton, and then meet with the cook to establish the menu for lunch and dinner. Next, she donned her garden apron, collected her basket and tools, and stepped from the front door of Estevan Lodge on her way for an inspection tour of the gardens. She would seek out Wyndham Coffin, the head gardener, to discuss the work to be undertaken, or that had already been accomplished, that day. Elsie worked in the gardens, sometimes picking flowers, sometimes planting. Secateurs in hand, trowel at the ready, she was a gardener on the prowl. When large projects were underway, she would hover near the men, surveying the heavy work and taking part in the planting or division of plants. At 1:15 p.m., Ernest Bufton would emerge from the house and ring the ship's bell, calling her for lunch – usually a light meal – which would be served in the dining room. Afterward,

Elsie and her gardeners planting
The Long Walk.

A silver bowl displays a spring bouquet.

Elsie Reford returned to the gardens and would work until tea at 4 p.m. Tea would fre-quently be taken on the veranda, sometimes alone, often with guests. After tea, she would retreat to her upstairs rooms and reappear with her husband, dressed for dinner, later in the evening. Dinner was served late to accommodate the fishing guests who rarely left the river until just before dusk. Dinner at Estevan Lodge was formal, with long evening dresses for women and black tie for men. The only exception was on Sundays when less formal attire prevailed – men were allowed to wear jacket and tie. Those who trespassed on convention were dealt with harshly. Once when her brother-in-law, sur-geon and *bon vivant* Dr. Lewis Reford, appeared late after a long and successful fight to land a salmon, Elsie Reford refused to let him sit down for dinner. Rules were rules. There were no exceptions.

At Estevan, Elsie Reford and her husband had a large staff at their service, reduced in comparison with the Drummond Street contingent, but still numerous. From the 1920s onwards, the head of the household staff was Ernest Bufton. Born and trained in Eng-land, Bufton (butlers were invariably referred to by their last names as an acknowledge-ment of their superior position in the domestic hierarchy) had served in the First World War before being hired by the Refords and arriving in Canada in 1921. A butler in what was essentially an Edwardian establishment had multiple responsibilities. He was charged with the most important duties in the service of his employers. In addition, he was responsible for the staff as a whole. He established the schedule, detailed working hours and holidays, and paid staff members. Bufton was charged with getting fresh, crisp bills from the bank every week, but Elsie Reford insisted on writing the names of each employee on their pay envelope. He was also responsible for maintaining staff decorum and household etiquette. Bufton dealt with suppliers and ensured deliveries. His personal duties included sorting the mail and polishing the silver. Bufton's own love

Elsie Reford with the Governor-General, Lord Grey, during his first visit to Estevan in 1906.

Bruce Reford, Elsie's eldest son, relaxing in the family car.

of nature was on display at Estevan. He created exotic centrepieces for the dining-room table on special occasions, using the flowers, plants and mosses that he collected and painstakingly assembled.

In addition to Bufton, the staff included Norman Hansen, a footman who worked in both Montreal and Metis. The footman assisted the butler with various household obligations, particularly in serving meals. The kitchen staff consisted of a cook and a scullery maid, who helped out and did the washing up. The upstairs staff included a lady's maid, whose primary responsibility was to assist Elsie Reford. She laid out and folded her clothes. She prettied the room and kept it tidy, even if there was little to tidy up. Elsie Reford was not one to leave things lying about. There was a laundress to do the daily washing and ironing of the linens. Elsie Reford's lady's maid doubled as a seamstress, repaired clothing and embroidered the linens with their distinctive Metis signature.

Since it was not uncommon for men who grew up in Montreal in the 1900s to be unable to drive and to rely on others for that purpose, the Refords kept a chauffeur in Montreal and another in Metis. In Metis, the chauffeur took pride in the McLaughlin Buick that he polished and kept in immaculate condition. Built in the 1920s, the car had three rows of seats, each with its own windscreen. It rarely escaped notice when its sleek silhouette was seen traversing the country roads and hills near the gardens, taking Elsie Reford and her guests for long, dusty drives to admire views from the hills above and behind the village of St. Octave.

The other key staff member was Wyndham Coffin, who worked at Grand-Metis for many years. Originally from Gaspé, his father had been a guide on the river for Lord Mount Stephen before him. He was offered the job of head gardener as Elsie Reford's confi-

Haymaking in front of Estevan Lodge.

The road to Estevan.

dence in his ability developed. He lived on the grounds, occupying the "guardian's cottage," built at the same time as Estevan Lodge, and raised his family there. After Elsie Reford left the property, he remained in the employ of Bruce Reford, staying on after the government of Quebec acquired the gardens in 1961, providing invaluable assistance as the province readied the gardens for public access in June 1962. One of his first requests at that time was the purchase of a garden tractor – Elsie Reford had never permitted such noisy machines in her gardens.

For the domestic staff, the daily ritual of serving the Refords was maintained throughout the summer. The household staff worked seven days a week. Bufton's day was 14 hours long – he had every other Friday afternoon and Sunday off. Mrs. Reford made a habit of giving staff picnics two or three times every summer, weather permitting. But the fishing guides worked every day without exception. When they were not guiding, they repaired the rods and canoes and patrolled the river on the lookout for poachers.

Two weeks before the Refords travelled down at the beginning of the summer, the staff were sent ahead to prepare the house. The servants arrived by train at Ste. Flavie Station (Mont-Joli) and were met by Mr. Coffin in a horse and buggy. It was Coffin's job to make sure the house was stocked with food. Bufton supervised the work of opening the house, removing the dust cloths, supervising the cleaning of the walls and floors, warming the house and readying the rooms for the Refords' arrival. In the early years, the stables were disinfected in preparation for Elsie Reford's horse, "Rocket," which was sent to Metis for the summer. Elsie loved to ride. Seated gracefully on Rocket, her silhouette was a familiar sight to locals who watched her ride along the beach or pass by on the dirt roads of the backcountry.

Once the house was ready, Elsie took the train from Montreal. In the early years she would arrive in June, but as her garden developed she turned up earlier and earlier, barely able to contain her excitement at seeing the garden as soon as it emerged from the snows. Her husband travelled by train on weekends in June and July and then spent several weeks in August, when the hot sultry weather in Montreal led him to flee the city for the cool, clean air of the Lower St. Lawrence. After retiring from the shipping business in the 1940s, he would spend the entire summer at Metis with his wife and their guests.

In 1926, Elsie Reford invited the Montreal architect, Galt Durnford, to design an addition to Estevan Lodge. A grandson of Colonel Elias Walker Durnford, the Royal Engineer who had designed and constructed the Citadel in Quebec City between 1820 and 1831, Galt Durnford had studied architecture at McGill University. He practised in Montreal with the firm of Featherstonhaugh and Durnford and was best known for the stone residences he designed for wealthy clients in Westmount. Estevan was one of his first projects, and his brief was to add rooms to the second storey. He designed an addition to be inserted into the existing structure.

Although large in size, the building was unable to accommodate excessively large parties. One of the reasons for Elsie Reford's 1926 addition was to provide more spacious and private quarters for her husband and herself. Family and guests could then be accommodated on the ground floor, while the Refords had the upper floor to themselves. Elsie sought to make Estevan more commodious for everyone. With her two boys married, she wanted them to have space for their wives and growing families. She also craved the privacy she enjoyed in Montreal, where her rooms and those of guests and visitors were on separate floors. A number of features were added to make the house

A
Day in
Paradise

85

Elsie Reford's Home, Montreal

The front door and balustrade were salvaged from Elsie's Drummond Street home by the McCord Museum of Canadian History in Montreal.

Before the house was broken up and the contents sold or dispersed, a series of photographs were taken, preserving Elsie and Robert Reford's Drummond Street residence for posterity.

The Reford family crest shows a gryphon with the motto "vrai et fort," a play on the pronunciation of Reford.

The fireplace from the dining room of Drummond Street.

The Reford Gardens

The demolition of Elsie Reford's house on Drummond Street in 1968 was just one of the many losses suffered by Montreal's architectural heritage in the 1960s and 1970s. While it endured the same fate as many of the historic homes in the city's Square Mile, the fact that it made way for a parking lot was an ignominious end for a house designed and built with the utmost care.

Elsie and Robert Wilson Reford's home was located at the top of Drummond Street (recently renamed Sir William Osler Way in honour of the famous doctor and medical educator), the last section of the street below the mountain. When it was built in 1900, it stood in a quiet corner of the Square Mile. Later, in 1954, the City of Montreal extended McGregor Street (now Wilder-Penfield Avenue) through the garden, transforming the exclusive neighbourhood into a chaotic boulevard.

From their own house, Elsie and Robert Wilson Reford could see several other family homes. Robert Reford's parents lived down the street in the old Torrance mansion. Dr. Lewis Reford and his wife, Jean, lived across the street, in a house demolished to make way for McGregor Street. Elsie's parents lived in George Stephen's mansion, between De Maisonneuve Blvd. and St. Catherine Street, until the building was sold to become the Mount Stephen Club in 1926.

The building of her home on Drummond Street was a project which enthralled both Elsie and her husband. It was designed by Robert Findlay, a Scottish-born and trained architect who practised in Montreal from 1885 onwards. For the Refords he built a three-storey house in brick and red sandstone. Facing south, the house had large rooms looking out over the city. There were 35 rooms.

VRAI ET FORT

Elsie and Robert Wilson Reford's Montreal residence at 3510 Drummond Street in the 1950s. From left to right, the Gallery, the façade and the Front Hall.

As clients, Findlay found the Refords an exhausting pair, as they were both fastidious and demanding. Records show that Elsie and Robert Reford selected every item for the house with care and discernment. They ordered silk for the walls in Paris, sconces in New York, and the hardware in the United Kingdom.

Little survives today. The house was broken up after Elsie Reford's death in 1967. The furniture was distributed or sold. The collection of books was shared by family members or found their way onto the shelves of dealers. Robert Reford's Canadiana collection was sold by Sotheby's – their first Canadian sale – taking three full days to be auctioned in May 1968 and attracting 15,000 visitors. The coins were auctioned in London and the medals in New York. What was not sold was given to the National Archives in Ottawa.

The wreckers sold the wood panelling to adorn a country house in the Laurentians. All that remains of the house today are photographs of the interior, taken by a professional photographer at the invitation of Elsie Reford in the 1950s. Several parts of the house were salvaged, such as the front door and the fireplace, both of which were donated to the McCord Museum of Canadian History in Montreal and which occasionally form part of their exhibitions.

This fireplace came from the dining room of the Reford House. The beautiful mantel is of mahogany, carved by hand, with leaves and grapes elegantly intertwined. At the centre is a copper and iron hood, the copper hammered and intricately carved. The entire ensemble is in the Art Nouveau style, but shows a classic restraint, suitable for the Refords' own taste, which tended to the traditional.

The Reford Gardens

Elsie and Eric Reford with the family dogs.

Elsie and Bruce.

Elsie Reford with her two boys. Eric was destined to run the family business and his older brother Bruce was a soldier. He was reputed to be the tallest man in the British Army for most of his career.

more comfortable. She created bedrooms and en suite bathrooms for herself and her husband. She also indulged their respective hobbies by adding a darkroom and a sewing room. Central heating was installed in her private quarters to provide comfort in the cooler days of spring and fall. Among the modifications made to Estevan Lodge was the addition of four chimneys, including one to service the fireplaces in Elsie's bedroom and sitting room. In the rooms added to the north side of the house, the Refords gave specific instructions for the interior millwork. The walls were to be panelled with red gum wood, a kind of eucalyptus that her husband imported from Australia. The balance of the woodwork was to be of B.C. fir like the original panelling. The new cedar-shingle roof was stained in the same oxblood colour as the original. The designs were completed in 1926 and the work executed in 1927 at a cost of $30,003.

Visitors to Grand-Metis were few, but once on the scene they were accorded special attention. Preferential treatment was reserved for Elsie Reford's two boys, who had been away at an English boarding school. When they returned to Canada in June, a mother's longing quickly gave way to maternal affection. Bruce and Eric disembarked from the Cunard or Canadian Pacific liner by pilot boat at nearby Father Point (Pointe-au-Père) and made their way directly to Estevan. Activities, excursions and expeditions were planned and carried out with military precision. They spent the summer with their mother, fishing, riding and shooting targets in the bay below the gardens. They built camps and "roughed it" overnight in the woods along the Mitis River. On one memorable occasion, they accompanied her on a two-week expedition, traversing the Gaspé peninsula on horseback. To celebrate their father's birthday on August 14, they organized an annual cookout at Pointe-aux-Cenelles, where Reford *père* abandoned the elaborate menus served at Estevan and cooked potatoes in the sand under a driftwood fire on the beach.

Bruce and Eric playing chess on the veranda.

Robert William Reford.

As they grew older and their visits became rarer, return journeys to Metis took on even greater significance. Eric Reford had his own summerhouse on Lake Memphremagog in Quebec's Eastern Townships and Bruce Reford lived in England. So when they came back, with their new spouses and later with Elsie's grandchildren, all the stops were pulled out. In his memoir, *Metis Memories*, my uncle, Robert Reford, has reminisced about arriving at the gardens as a young boy on one of his summer holidays spent at Grand-Metis in the 1930s:

> "Coming in from the road, there were the white gates leading to a gently curving driveway, lined with spruce trees. In front of the house, a large clump of cedar trees had been planted in a circle. As they grew up, they were known as the Boule, and they virtually concealed the building until you were right up to the entrance.
>
> Waiting to greet us was my Grandmother. She was immaculately dressed, in a style entirely appropriate for a 'grande dame' in a country setting. She was always clearly in charge, always with a formal approach, and she showered affection on me as the eldest son of her eldest son. The servants would be on hand, taking our luggage from the car, carrying it to our rooms."

Once settled, they would spend the first of many days on the river. The ritual of fishing had its own rhythm. Generally, two to four rods would be on the river at any one time. For those whose day began on the river, a light breakfast was laid out in the dining room. They would be taken upriver in horse and buggy, or in a car in later years, to the Mill Falls where the road to the village of Price ran close to the Mitis River. They would walk to the river with the rods and fishing gear and begin the morning's fishing, embarking in a canoe with a guide at both bow and stern. The Gaspé canoes (with flat

bottoms and wide gunnels) were poled downriver from pool to pool, the guides positioning the canoes to allow the fishermen access to the pools and the salmon hidden within. Wherever there were rapids, the guides left the fishermen on the riverbanks and negotiated the rocks and rapids, collecting them lower down. Most of the fishing on the Mitis River was done from canoes, only occasionally from the shore where, as at the Rock Pool, the fish could be landed from the bank. The morning was organized to ensure that the canoes arrived at the anchorage below Estevan Lodge, trophy in hand, in time for lunch. Successes or failures provided an opportunity to regale the hostess and her visitors with fishing yarns. The ritual would be repeated in late afternoon, when the salmon awakened from their afternoon slumber and would again rise to the fly cast carefully in the pools. The fish caught would be immediately placed in ice from the icehouse. Many found their way to the dining-room table. Others were given to villagers or sent to friends by train in ice-packed wooden boxes. Each fisherman would weigh his fish on the scales next to Estevan Lodge, then note the pool, conditions, and fly used, in the fishing book. These books record every fish caught on the Mitis River from 1908 to 1942. Elsie Reford's own record was a 43-pound salmon that she caught in 1912. On July 12, 1942 the Refords took the last salmon on the Mitis River. That day, Robert Wilson Reford and his grandson, Boris, caught salmon of 24 pounds and 22 pounds respectively. Their kills were duly recorded in the fishing book.

Elsie Reford entertained more than just her own family. She carried on the tradition, established by her uncle, of hosting the Governor-General and his staff. In 1906 she invited Lord Grey and his wife, Lady Sybil, to stay and to fish on the Mitis River. It was the beginning of an intense friendship between herself and Lord Grey that ended only with his death in 1917. Grey was just one of many governors-general who visited Estevan, either to fish or simply to enjoy the beauties and pleasures of the region. Those

The icehouse and water tower, circa 1920.

Eric Reford with his catch of the day.

Salmon were occasionally sent by train to friends and family in ice-packed boxes.

The Mitis River.

Fresh Fish: Forward at Once
ONE SALMON

| From
THE GRAND METIS RIVER | Weight | lbs. |

Compliments of Mrs. R. W. REFORD

The gardens in spring.

Elsie and a friend in the cutting garden.

Robert and Elsie with their dog, Peter, on The Long Walk.

that followed included Lord Bessborough, Lord Tweedsmuir and the Earl of Athlone and his wife, Princess Alice. Guests even pitched in on occasion. In July 1945, Princess Alice was put to work in the garden. She toiled alongside Elsie Reford for most of her visit.

Vice-Regal visits imposed a protocol that was foreign even to Elsie's rigid standards. Planning and orchestration were required on a grand scale. Letters and telegrams would speed to and from Ottawa discussing the minutest details. Receiving the Governor-General required a thorough housecleaning, polishing of the silver, and the removal of staff to accommodate the Governor-General's own contingent. It also imposed rituals on the family. Remembering a visit from the Earl of Bessborough in 1935, my uncle has written:

> "His presence involved protocol to an extraordinary degree. I was instructed to bow when I was introduced to him, to speak only when spoken to, and to call him Your Excellency. As a special privilege for the eldest grandchild, I was invited to join the party for dinner. Here was a whole new set of rules: Do not start eating until he does, stop eating when he has finished even if you still have more food on your plate, rise for the toast to the Monarch. As a 14-year-old, I found the formality tiresome, but I accepted that it was necessary for the King's representative in Canada.

Elsie was not always enthusiastic about visitors, in particular about what accompanied them. When the Tessiers, a prominent Rimouski family, arrived in 1911 in the company of Sir Alexandre Lacoste, then chief justice of Quebec, and his wife, she wrote: "It is terrible to think of motors descending upon us here," adding, "but I quite enjoyed their visit." Drivers were under strict orders to proceed at low speeds along the driveway, so the plants would not be covered in dust. Every Saturday morning the entire drive was raked in order to keep the dust at a minimum.

Elsie leading a visit to the gardens.

Elsie often ventured into the backcountry near the gardens, admiring the hilly country behind the village of St. Octave.

The ritual of gardening added to the daily regimen. Rarely a day went by without Elsie Reford recording her work. While she was an unabashed amateur, she nonetheless understood that horticulture required a methodology. "Unless the amateur gardener is unusually persevering in keeping accurate records," she wrote, "he or she has little to offer by way of assistance to others when it comes to passing on more or less scientific information regarding the elements and conditions which have contributed to their particular achievements." Her daily ritual can be examined from the thousands of diary pages that she kept so assiduously over more than 30 years. Sixty years ago, Elsie's husband remarked to his cousin Christina Drummond: "My wife's garden is better than ever. She works in it from morning to night and after dinner tackles her correspondence till midnight."

Only when external events intervened did Elsie reglect to enter the day's activities in her diary, helping us to understand that beneath the austere exterior there lurked an emotional woman. She was unable to write when concern over the fate of her son and grandchildren during the war years almost immobilized her. One such moment occurred on September 1, 1939, the day that German troops invaded Poland, making war in Europe inevitable. Her garden diary ends, "...All reserves have been called to the colours and all men between 18 and 41 will be liable for service. It makes one heartsick – but everyone will be ready for duty. The joy gone out of garden work but must carry on meanwhile." When her eldest son, Bruce, was part of the British Expeditionary Force trapped in France by the advancing German army in May 1940, her diary notes, "...All report the British force under Lord Gort in the most perilous position and fighting desperately to retire either to Dunkirk or to reach the main French army...We hold our breath for what each hour a day may bring forth. Meanwhile nature unconcerned has gone on doing her best for beauty in the world and the gardens have been coming on

The first dusting of snow.

Crab apple (*Malus* cv.) blossom.

Teak benches donated by friends of the gardens provide places of rest for visitors.

The gardens are home to more than 90 crab apples, which provide glorious, if fleeting, bloom in June.

wonderfully." Bruce Reford escaped from Dunkirk in one of the hundreds of small boats rallied for that miraculous evacuation. A telegram confirmed his safe arrival in England, ending her anxiety.

Estevan's peace was disturbed in other ways. In 1941, the construction of airfields for the bombing and gunnery school of the British Commonwealth Air Training Plan on fields north of Mont-Joli (site of the present Mont-Joli airport) made the area buzz with activity. As part of the military installations, the Royal Canadian Air Force leased the Pointe aux Cenelles opposite the gardens and used the reef as the site for target practice. The sky above Estevan Lodge was thick with aircraft for much of the war. Gas rationing also led the Refords to sell their hunting camp, Cariboo, on a lake 40 miles to the southwest. For 40 years, they had trekked to the cabin in the fall and winter, exploring the beauties of the region and enjoying its rustic simplicity. Without fuel, they could no longer make the cross-country expedition to reach the camp. After its sale, their enjoyment of the region was limited to the summer months.

The upkeep of Estevan Lodge entailed a significant financial burden. Even before she built the garden, Elsie Reford's account book shows that she spent $9,587 on wages, house expenditures, and the automobile in 1923. After garden construction had begun, her staff swelled, as did the cost of running the property. There was Coffin, the guardian and head gardener, and three or four extra men in the gardens. James Pearce was in charge of the vegetable garden, where he put his training at Edinburgh's Royal Botanic Garden to good use. Add to them, Douglas Berchervaise and Lewis Eden, Gaspémen who guided on the river, as well as three or four other guides and guardians who helped out during the height of the summer. On the farms, there were both tenants and farmhands, tilling the fields, cutting the hay, and feeding the chickens, sheep, dairy and beef cattle.

Elsie Goes Hunting

Fishing was Elsie Reford's sport of choice, but this did not prevent her from hunting on occasion. Indeed, the first property she and her husband owned in the Lower St. Lawrence was a woodland camp that they baptized Cariboo after the name of the lake near which it was built, south of Rimouski. It was there, in the early 1900s, when they first came to hunt during the fall and winter months.

Robert Reford admitted that his wife was not a dedicated hunter. But we know that she did shoot at least one caribou. In 1906, her husband made the hoof of that specimen into a commemorative inkwell. That Elsie could also handle a firearm is illustrated by the 1909 bronze statuette by Louis-Philippe Hébert. Entitled *À l'affût*, the statuette was a gift from her husband. It shows Elsie Reford, rifle in hand, with a floppy hat not unlike the one she wore at Cariboo on their trips there together.

Elsie herself was not exactly enamoured of the bronze, referring to it as "this thing Hébert did of me." She said that "all my friends say the face is very bad" and joked that her husband had photographed the view he liked best – the one from the rear! The statuette is similar in many ways to Hébert's well-known Madeleine de Verchères. Hébert produced the smaller version of the Madeleine de Verchères in 1905.

Years later, Elsie Reford instigated the erection of a memorial to Madeleine. According to an article by E.Z. Massicotte in *La Presse*, published in 1910, "A year ago, an English-speaking woman from Montreal, Mrs. Robert Reford, acquired a statuette of Marie-

"My days in the woods were beyond expression beautiful. Nature clad in her soft white garments for her long rest with not even the tiniest tinkle of a bird note to break the silence is a different nature from the green clad nature throbbing with growth and life. Even one's own footsteps on snowshoes over the soft snow were inaudible and oh the joy of freedom in breaking one's own tracks up over mountains and across lakes. The night we left camp at 6 p.m. the new moon was just rising and the road and then three hours driving along a country road without meeting a living soul."

Elsie Reford to Lord Grey, January 12, 1911

Madeleine de Verchères, executed by that most distinguished of Quebec sculptors, Mr. Philippe Hébert. Mrs. Reford was amazed that this remarkable and heroic historical figure, so vividly captured by the artist, had been allowed to fall into total obscurity. There was not a single inscription, let alone a monument, to commemorate a feat of arms for which other countries admired our history. Then and there, this lady, English-speaking at that, determined to organize a campaign to reverse the mood of long-running ingratitude and oversight which had befallen the pure heroine." Elsie enlisted the support of Lord Grey, who in turn convinced the Canadian prime minister, Sir Robert Borden, to put up a monument in Madeleine's honour. In 1913 it was erected in Verchères, overlooking the St. Lawrence River, and remains the largest bronze statue in Canada, at 22 feet in height and weighing 4½ tons.

"From its position on a high cliff over-hanging the St. Lawrence the ground slopes away irregularly, sometimes gently, sometimes sharply until it takes a precipitous descent to the brook, which winds it way through the entire property, singing as it hurries gleefully down to the sea. It is thus obvious that the lay of the land creates many different levels with excellent drainage on the slopes between them; there are banks low and high, steep or of easy grade and all have been made use of for lilies but ever with the greatest care taken not to interfere, under any circumstances, with natural pitch."

Elsie Reford, *A Lily Garden in the Lower St. Lawrence Valley*

The Azalea Garden.

Life at Grand–Metis changed substantially after Elsie Reford sold the lower reaches of the Mitis River to the Lower St. Lawrence Power Company in 1942. She had sold the falls to the same company more than 20 years earlier. Controlled by Jules Brillant, a brilliant and successful local entrepreneur, the power company provided electricity to the entire Gaspé peninsula by means of the small dam built on the Mitis River in the early 1920s. Under pressure from Brillant, and the threat of expropriation due to the wartime need for increased hydroelectric power, she sold the rest of the river. But she did so reluctantly and under duress. She knew that a second dam on the river would flood the pools and put an end both to the salmon spawning grounds and to salmon fishing itself. While she deeply regretted the sale, and resented even more the political manoeuvring which she felt had conspired to deprive her of her legacy, she negotiated long and hard with Jules Brillant's lawyers and engineers to cede as little property as possible and to get the best price for her prized asset.

The sale of the river also ended the rights and duties that Elsie Reford had assumed as the seigneur of the area. The seigniorial regime in Quebec was created by the French Crown as a means of settling and developing the vast territories of New France. Seigneurs were granted seigneuries by the Crown, providing them with tracts of land, complete with timber and fishing rights. In return, the seigneur was obliged to provide a mill for the local community and ensure the settlement of his lands. While the Pachot fief and the De Peiras seigneurie which Elsie Reford inherited from her uncle had never been settled during the French regime, and the seigniorial rights had been abolished by the government of Lower Canada in 1854, the old seigneuries carried a certain mystique and a sense of noblesse oblige. When she first took up residence in her uncle's fishing camp, the local priest dubbed her "La Dame de la Grande Maison Blanche – the Lady of the Metis Castle." And Elsie Reford took her responsibilities seriously. She provided

The view from St. Octave, then and now.

The road to the mouth of the Mitis River.

assistance to the poorest families in the village and employed local men wherever possible. After the stock market crash in 1929 and the economic difficulties that followed, she redoubled her efforts, providing fresh salmon caught in the river and making gifts of food and clothing to the poorest residents. Her gardeners came from families who lived nearby, particularly the Larivées and the Cassistas. She found their natural understanding of plants and capacity for hard work more than compensation for a lack of formal training. Elsie Reford paid well, but not extravagantly. And unlike many other women of her age, she played an active role in the management of her own finances. She paid the employees in the gardens and on the river from her own funds. Her husband took responsibility for the farms and the sale of animals and produce.

An astute observer of politics and the community, Elsie Reford was adept at understanding her role in the region. She cultivated amicable relations with the important members of the community, such as the *curé* of the local parish or the manager of the Price Brothers lumber mill in nearby Price. She made modest donations to various causes and gave prizes to the students in the school in Grand-Metis. She was revered by local families who received gifts, left without ceremony, at their front doors. Girls selling berries or *Capitaine* Lionel Deroy with his catch of smelts were never turned away. The staff had a standing order to purchase their harvest. She even provided a bounty for boys, encouraging them to hunt the moles that undermined her gardens and dug up her pristine lawns. But she objected when local politicians interfered in what she felt to be her private business. More than once she thwarted attempts to develop a fishery in the bay of the Mitis River. She held Jules Brillant to the letter of the law so far as the clauses in their contract were concerned, protecting the river from oil spills and keeping the water at an established level regardless of hydroelectric production. Poachers were dealt with harshly and immediately subjected to the full hammer of the law. And while she had

"Snow remains longer on the ground at Grand Metis than it does in Montreal or Ottawa, hence the spring awakening is about a fortnight later than it is in those cities. The scourge of late spring frosts is practically unknown to the Estevan Lilies, they never push through until nature has made it quite safe for them. The depth of the snow-fall naturally varies with different seasons and may be anything from 3 feet over all to 4 or 5 feet, as in this last winter, and even up to 10 and 12 feet in the drifts."

Elsie Reford, *Lilies at Estevan Lodge*

Hemerocallis lilioasphodelus (syn. H. Flava).

Pages 112-113 : Black-eyed Susan (*Rudbeckia hirta* cv.).

Pages 114-115 : Francine Larivée's *Un paysage dans le paysage – le paysage comme tableau vivant, 1993-1996* is a masterpiece of the integration of contemporary art in a historic setting.

many friends in nearby Little Metis (Metis-sur-Mer), she rarely ventured forth to partic-ipate in the active social and community life there. Estevan was as self-sufficient as its owner.

A day in paradise brought Elsie Reford a host of pleasures. But the responsibilities were also legion. At day's end, she was justifiably proud of her achievements. Her handiwork had transformed the rustic surroundings of Estevan Lodge into a horticultural paradise. And the simple fishing lodge had become a home and the lifeblood for dozens in the surrounding community.

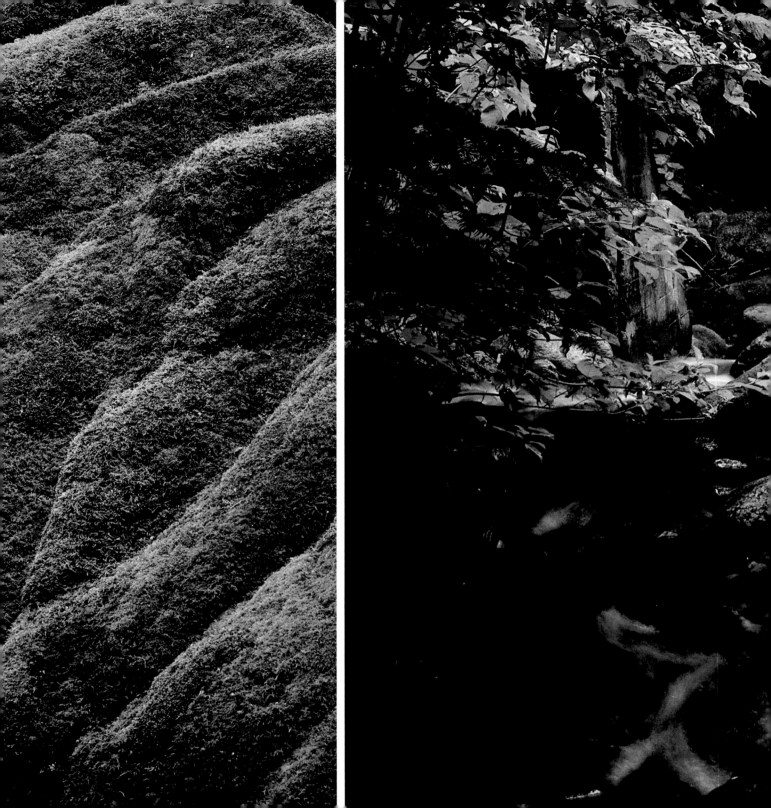

CHAPTER 4

"Lilacs were marvellous, azaleas very brilliant but I sometimes wonder if the sweeps of blue poppies are not the most satisfying, for apart from their great beauty they outlast everything else for length of time of flowering. They have now been giving much delight for almost a month."

Elsie Reford, July 13, 1954

Pages 116-117:
View of the High Bank.

Pages 118-119:
In the beauty of the lilies.

Himalayan blue poppy
(Meconopsis betonicifolia).

A Tapestry of Wondrous Beauty

Elsie Reford was a collector. She collected paintings, *objets d'art* and jewellery. Throughout the 1920s, she and her husband frequented art dealers in London and New York. They assembled one of the finest collections of European paintings in Montreal. When they travelled, their days were carefully planned around gallery tours, visits to dealers and return trips to the shops they had patronized for decades. It comes as no surprise, therefore, that Elsie was also a collector when it came to plants.

Now, there are plant collectors who garden, and gardeners who collect plants. Elsie Reford was someone who both gardened and collected. A collector's garden is often very different from an ornamental garden. Plants are often grouped by species or varieties with little or no regard for the basic elements of garden design, such as colour, height and blooming period. But while Elsie collected plants, she did so with an eye to amplifying their beauty by careful placement. At Estevan, Elsie amassed more than half-a-dozen collections: lilies, meconopsis, gentians, roses, peonies and primula that rivalled those of many other gardens on the continent.

For this reason alone, Elsie Reford is considered a pioneer of Canadian gardening. When she first began, there was still a widespread conviction that many perennials could not survive the Canadian climate. The belief relied more on myth than experience. Canadian gardeners had long laboured under the mistaken notion that the early frosts, short

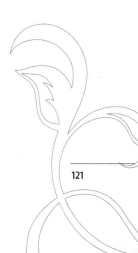

121

The Reford Madonna

Over the course of her long life, Elsie Reford was fascinated by paintings and by Italy. For this reason, perhaps, she was seduced into buying a painting of a Madonna and child in 1928. When the Refords bought it — from the New York art dealer Wildenstein for $10,000 — the work was attributed to Sodoma (Giovanni Antonio Bazzi), a minor sixteenth-century Italian master. The couple proved to be prescient, since the painting, previously owned by Lord Battersea, had been identified as a Leonardo da Vinci, and even exhibited as such at the Burlington Fine Arts Club in London. Intrigued, Elsie and Robert Reford spent many years trying to establish its authenticity. Leonardo made few paintings, and almost all of them have been in public collections since the 19th century.

Elsie and Robert Reford encouraged art experts to visit their Montreal home to view the painting and confirm its attribution. The first was W.H. Valentiner, the director of the Art Institute of Chicago, one of America's leading museums. He confirmed the Leonardo attribution. Another expert, the German art historian Wilhelm Suida, compared it favourably to the *Madonna of the Yarnwinder*, in the possession of the Duke of Buccleuch, a premier Scottish landowner and holder of one of the world's great collections. The duke's Madonna was more widely accepted to be by the hand of Leonardo.

Interest in the painting grew after it was shown at the New York World's Fair Exhibition in 1939. But after Elsie Reford's death, the dealers who had so enthusiastically endorsed the attribution in the 1930s recanted. When the family decided to sell the painting in the 1970s, no buyers could be found. Wildenstein bought it back at auction in 1971, but for a sum less than the Refords had paid 40 years earlier. The dealer then sold the painting to a New York collector who still owns it and has spent almost 30 years working at its authentication.

The so-called Reford Madonna was shown at the Leonardo exhibition held in the Tuscan town of Vinci, Italy, in 1982 and at the National Gallery of Scotland in 1992, alongside the Buccleuch Madonna. The exhibition's curator, Dr. Martin Kemp, a leading Leonardo expert, wrote in the catalogue that the painting almost certainly originated in Leonardo's studio and that it was painted under the supervision of the great master himself, perhaps even executed by him.

It is unlikely, however, that the paintings will ever be exhibited together again — at least in the short term. The Buccleuch Madonna was stolen from the duke's Scottish home, Drumlanrig Castle, on August 28, 2003. Valued at more than $ 40 million (US), the painting has not yet resurfaced, and may never be seen again.

Portrait of Elsie Reford by P.A. de László, 1915.

The studio in the Refords' Montreal residence.

Interior of Estevan Lodge.

The Reford Madona.

The Reford Gardens

'Avant Garde' peony.

Miniature plant adorning an old millstone.

Pincushion flower (*Scabiosa caucasia*).

White turkscap lilies (*Lilium martagon* var. *album*).

Primula vialii.

growing season and cold winters were fatal to perennials. So they tended to content themselves with annuals and brightly coloured bedding plants that had been the rage of the Victorian era. Parks and public gardens still displayed these floral tableaux long after serious gardeners and collectors had begun to experiment with more exotic perennials. Little experimentation had been conducted on perennials in Canada to prove their hardiness. The travails of trial and error were reserved for the foolish or the courageous. Writing for the members of the North American Lily Society, Elsie admitted to being both: "...it is hoped that enough may have been said for members to realize that lilies can be grown where snows and severe winters have fewer disadvantages than sometimes believed. Their cultivation, like that of all else in the gardens, has been learned the old hard way – by trial and error."

Elsie Reford was among those who benefited from the great advances in horticulture during the early 1900s. In Canada, the experimental farms created by Sir John A. Macdonald's government across the country in the 1880s had developed breeding programs for cereals, wheat, potatoes, fruit trees and other agricultural crops. By the 1890s, hybridizers at the experimental farms turned their attention to ornamental plants, beginning experiments with hardy perennials for Canadian gardens. Their results were remarkable and quickly made an impact in Canada. Varieties and cultivars of lilacs, ornamental crab apples, lilies and roses were among the plants introduced to Canadian gardeners, and those around the world, between 1900 and 1930 as a result of the hybridizers' research. By using her network of contacts and her attentive reading of horticultural publications, Elsie was among the first to obtain the experimental hybrids, sometimes even before they were available commercially. In this sense, Elsie Reford's is very much a Canadian garden. She proudly displayed hybrids developed expressly for her native climate.

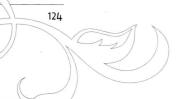

But her supply network was not limited to Canadian nurseries. It spanned the globe. The era was one of intense plant exploration. Many of the plants of Asian origin that we grow in our gardens today were "discovered" by plant explorers in this period, then introduced to gardening and gardeners. Elsie was interested in the latest discoveries or hybrids, following reports of their availability with almost giddy enthusiasm.

Early on, she showed a particular passion for lilies. Her affection for "these peerless flowers" was so strong that she routinely described her garden as a "lily garden in the Lower St. Lawrence valley." While lilies are readily available today, we forget that many are fairly recent introductions. This explains why Elsie Reford could write of "adventuring with Lilies" when she first began planting them in the 1920s:

> "The word 'adventuring' is used in a literal sense, for with the exception of an odd clump of *Lilium tigrinum* to be seen here and there in tiny vegetable gardens in the back country and a rare *L. candidum* (known in these parts as 'le lis de St. Joseph') growing in like circumstances, Lilies were quite unknown in this section of the Province of Quebec..." (*Lilies at Estevan Lodge*)

Lilies came into vogue in the early 1900s. While many species had been known for centuries, others were introduced by plant explorers active in China and Tibet in the late nineteenth and early twentieth centuries. The regal lily, *Lilium regale*, one of Elsie's favourites, was introduced to gardeners by the English plant explorer Ernest Henry "Chinese" Wilson, who sent home boxes of lily bulbs packed in clay on his fourth and last expedition to China in 1913. Like others, Elsie Reford was inspired by the influential English garden designer and writer, Gertrude Jekyll, whose book *Lilies for English Gardens*, published in 1901, encouraged many to grow lilies rather than simply display them in vases.

A Tapestry
of Wondrous
Beauty

"Now we come to the time when there is a veritable festival of Lily enchantment and it would be a courageous judge indeed who would submit that in sheer perfection any one variety could lead all the rest. In weight of numbers L. regale does outstrip the others — in the meantime — for they are in the thousands of blooms. The increase of this Lily through its bulblets has been tremendous, and, plant it where one will, in sun or shade, in acid or in alkaline soil, it does, grows tall and crowns itself with many blooms. Most effective of all are these L. regale on a steep bank along the brook, growing among many other 'lovely delights,' or in the long double sloping herbaceous border with its vista, through broken waves of their exquisite blooms rising one above the other out of masses of blending colourings, out to the blue hills beyond the sea; and before the approach of twilight, when the afterglow in rose and crimson, and blue and flame and purple and gold flows over all those waves of Lilies, faintly tinging every flower."

Elsie Reford, *Lilies at Estevan Lodge*

Lilium taliense var. Kaichen.

"*There has been no landscape architect to head off mistakes, costly in time and work to remedy but each one of them teaching something; there has been no trained gardener in the accepted meaning of the term; no one possessed of scientific botanical knowledge; but there have been a few young men who have worked ungrudgingly, taking little count of the hours, and with love of what they had to do. They have their reward when they see spread over the ground before them a tapestry of wondrous beauty – made with the help of their faithful, devoted labour – woven from flowers gay, brilliant and proud, timid and delicate and sweet, with roses the queens but lilies the benediction.*"

Elsie Reford, *A Lily Garden in the Lower St. Lawrence Valley*

Lilium 'Vivaldi'.

"The formula for any garden in the making has been a 3-foot trenching with 6 inches of large stones in the bottom and filled in with peat and sand in equal parts; leaf mould, fine gravel or lime grit or fertilizer being incorporated according to what may be the special requirement for the respective plantings. The depth of planting for the Lily bulbs has been guided by the general rule of one inch deeper than that given by the various growers from whom the bulbs have been obtained, except in the case of L. candidum and L. giganteum which have been put in quite as shallow as directed. Wood ash is scratched in round all Lilies when first they emerge from the ground in the spring."

Elsie Reford, *Lilies at Estevan Lodge*

Roses and lilies on The Long Walk combine to provide fragrance and beauty.

"A large proportion of the people who are taking a practical interest in horticulture," Jekyll wrote, "hardly as yet know one Lily from another."

My great-grandmother was one of the first in Canada to cultivate them on a large scale. And large scale it was. In September 1928, she planted 92 lily bulbs, the first of thousands she would add to the gardens over the years. Her order book illustrates a particular interest in species lilies, displaying as many as 60 of the 90 to 100 species found in the northern hemisphere. Attracted by their form and rarity, she was also intrigued by the apparent difficulty of raising them in Grand-Metis. To her surprise, they enjoyed the climate as much as she did. "In the clarity and purity of the atmosphere of the Lower St. Lawrence, in a garden where they have Spruce woods to shelter them and a running brook to sing to them Lilies do grow amazingly." Her collection ranged from the curvaceous white turkscap lily, *(Lilium martagon* var. *album)* to the golden-rayed lily *(Lilium auratum)* both beautiful and fragrant. Without question, their scent was one of the reasons that lilies so attracted her in the first place. "There rise in broken waves literally thousands of *Lilium regale* to waft their fragrance over the land," she wrote. So strong was the scent that on occasion she believed she could detect their presence while walking on the beach below the gardens, hundreds of feet away.

No collection is ever complete in the eyes of a devotee. There is thus a constant hunt for missing species or cultivars, the addition of the most recent hybrid or the search for an ever rarer specimen. "...Always there will be the desire to widen experience," she wrote, "and enrich still further this little corner of the world with treasures which nature, in her wisdom and generosity, has distributed elsewhere and to hail and welcome, as they come to us, the rewards of the patient work of the hybridizers."

"Between June 25 and 30 two Liliums open almost simultaneously; namely, L. Martagon album and L. umbellatum var. erectum. Both grow vigorously and well, the latter doing better in partial shade where it attains 4 feet with 6 to 8 flowers, whereas in sun it is more stunted in growth and has fewer flowers. L. Martagon album has in no instance come to its full beauty until four years after planting — but how well worth waiting for. A group, growing in a shady glen with Meconopsis betonicifolia in soil heavily enriched with leaf mould, produced a remarkable stem carrying 41 blooms and others with 20 to 30."

Elsie Reford, *Lilies at Estevan Lodge*

White turkscap lilies *(Lilium martagon* var. *album)* in bloom.

"Lilium speciosum, the type, and var. album Kractzeri, both so very lovely, are rather prone to ill health, and constant vigilance must be exercised. They must be grown in the hottest places in the gardens and in full sun, otherwise they will not open until too late in the season, and for us any time after early October is too late. By the end of that month the work for preparation against frost must be begun, so that their flowering brings to a close the time of happiness in the transcending beauty of the genus, so for all their gay appearance they introduce a feeling of sadness. Through long months ahead it is left to memory to try to gather back some of the delight of our Lilies and to imagination to frame pictures of yet greater beauty for the future."

Elsie Reford, *Lilies at Estevan Lodge*

The meadow lily *(Lilium canadense)* is one of our most beautiful native plants.

Elsie was among the first to obtain hybrids from Isabella Preston, the self-taught hybridizer who developed lily hybrids at the Ontario Agricultural College in Guelph and later at the Central Experimental Farm in Ottawa. Commenting on one of Preston's lilies, the *Lilium* 'George C. Creelman,' she wrote, "All lovers and growers of Lilies are laid under a debt of gratitude to Miss Isabella Preston for this splendid achievement in hybridization."

On occasion, we have succeeded where Elsie Reford failed. We have several large clumps of the beautiful and delicate meadow lily, *(Lilium canadense)*. Rarely seen in gardens, it is the only native lily. Elsie Reford described it with enthusiasm bordering on envy, its "lovely gold apricot orange bells swaying in the breeze," "its wonderful grace of poise, responding with a peculiar movement all its own, to the caress of every lightest movement in the air." Once found growing in the fields of Quebec and Ontario, it is not often seen in the wild. In cultivation, it enjoys wet, almost swampy conditions. But the Meadow Lily provided Elsie Reford with considerable frustration :

"Many other varieties of lilies thrive with us, but what of the failures, for there have been some. Oddly enough there has been a near failure with our native *L. canadense* growing to exquisite perfection in the valley of the Matapedia not much more than 100 miles distant. Bulbs were brought from there but after merely moderate growth for a couple of seasons with few flowers they did not re-appear. New bulbs were acquired from a nursery garden last autumn, instead of from the wild as heretofore, and the results eagerly looked forward to, for this lily has a peculiar charm and gracefulness that make it an adornment of any garden." (*A Lily Garden in the Lower St. Lawrence Valley*)

Tiger lily 'Sweet Surrender'
(Lilium tigrinum).

"It is a half revealed truth that gardeners, for the most part, differ from many of their fellow men in that success has at length crowned their efforts, whatever many have gone before, toil, trial, and error, disappointment, failures, all are swept completely from memory – obliterated in the ecstasy of pure joy at the sight of plants yielding up their loveliest rewards."

Elsie Reford, *Gentians at Estevan Lodge*

The Himalayan blue poppy (*Meconopsis betonicifolia*) is just one of the outstanding plants of Asiatic origin in the gardens' collection.

Her frustration is entirely understandable. The 100 bulbs she planted in September 1933 brought no results and her continued efforts to cultivate this species appear to have been thwarted.

Where there was failure, there was also success. One of Elsie Reford's proudest moments was her achievement with the giant Himalayan lily *(Cardiocrinum giganteum)*. So named because it can reach more than 12 feet in height, the Giant Lily is native to the rain forests of the Himalayas. Known to be difficult to grow, it takes as many as seven years from germination until it blooms. And after the plant blooms, it dies. Elsie Reford planted her first bulbs in 1938. The blooming of the *Cardiocrinum* was the garden event of the decade. She lived to see hers bloom on several occasions. Several photographs show Elsie Reford posing with her horticultural trophy, dwarfed by her achievement. Our attempts to repeat this garden event have thus far proved both fruitless and expensive.

The *Cardiocrinum* was not the only exotic Asian plant to whet her enthusiasm. For more than two decades, the signature plant of Les Jardins de Métis has been the Himalayan blue poppy *(Meconopsis betonicifolia)*. Its unique colour, pristine beauty, difficulty in growing and rarity, doubtless contributed to this choice. Its pure blue colour is also a marketer's dream. Today the gardens boast one of the largest collections of *Meconopsis betonicifolia* in the world.

The provenance of Elsie's *Meconopsis* provides an insight into her collecting skills. The Himalayan blue poppy is one of the marvels of the plant world. Native to the Tsangpo Gorge in Tibet's southeast corner, it grows at altitudes of 10,000 to 13,000 feet. The English plant explorer, Frank Kingdon Ward, who discovered the poppy in 1924, described its

Several hundred *Meconopsis grandis* have been planted in the woodland next to the site of the International Garden Festival. *Meconopsis grandis* has flowers which are larger and of a deeper blue hue than *M. betonicifolia*.

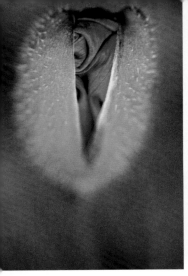

The Himalayan blue poppy blooms in mid-June and flowers until the end of July.

most outstanding characteristic: "...its flowers were flawless, of that intense almost luminous turquoise blue one associates with the clear atmosphere of the roof of the world." Ever since Ward presented his find to a meeting of the Royal Horticultural Society in London in 1926, the Himalayan blue poppy has enchanted and mesmerized gardeners. Intrigued by the enthusiasm that it generated, Elsie Reford was among the first North American gardeners to attempt growing the species. She obtained seeds from the Royal Botanic Gardens in Edinburgh in the 1930s. While not immediate, her success was considerable. By 1936, she had more than half-a-dozen species of *Meconopsis*, including *M. betonicifolia*, *M. grandis*, *M. integrifolia*, *M. napaulensis*, *M. quintuplinervia* and *M. simplicifolia*. A decade later, Frank Kingdon Ward told of receiving a letter of thanks "from a lady in Canada, enclosing a photograph showing hundreds of plants flowering in her garden on the shore of the St. Lawrence estuary. 'So well does it grow that to walk along a path between gently sloping banks entirely veiled with the exquisite blue poppies is like going through some ethereal valley in a land of dreams'." The "lady" was Elsie Reford.

Himalayan blue poppies present a challenge to gardeners. Unlike most poppies, they need rich and slightly acidic soil. They also thrive in cool summers and are barely resistant to drought or excessive temperatures. Gardeners in temperate regions like the Pacific Northwest have greater success with the blue poppy than those who live in warmer, dryer climates.

The microclimate at Grand-Metis is partly natural, partly created. Situated on a height of land, above the chill winds and waters of the St. Lawrence, the property is protected from the effects of the sea breeze and salt air. The Pointe aux Cenelles harbours Estevan from the winds that occasionally blow with ferocity from the north. Over time, Elsie Reford allowed a windbreak of spruce and poplar trees to grow. These trees shield the

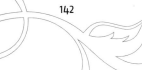

gardens and help keep snow on the plants for prolonged periods. Elsie planted the Himalayan blue poppies where the harsh winter conditions were moderated by the snow cover and the protection offered by the topography of the site.

At Estevan, the Himalayan blue poppies begin to bloom in mid-June. They are in flower through the month of July and sometimes into August, each plant producing a dozen or more flowers that bloom one after the other. Because blue is uncommon in the plant world, the Himalayan blue poppy is remarkable simply because of its unique colour. Nestled against the backdrop of common ferns and turkscap lilies, the Himalayan blue poppies are planted in a glade, shielded from the hot sun by conifers and the canopy of a crab apple tree. Regularly moistened by the rains common on the Lower St. Lawrence, the conditions at Grand-Metis are close to ideal.

Success with Himalayan blue poppies has long been one of the hallmarks in gardening. Those who grow them justifiably boast of their achievement. Moreover, success is defined not only in the cultivation, but also in the plant's germination. The seeds are difficult to find and often hard to germinate. To satisfy the interest of adventurous gardeners, the gardens' assistant director, Jean-Yves Roy, has successfully piloted the development of trial beds which today display more than 10,000 plants, progeny of the plants Elsie Reford began growing in the 1930s. The seeds are collected and dried and sold at the gardens. Plants are sold in the spring and fall. Few gardeners have equalled Elsie's success with the Himalayan blue poppy. But her example shows that even the most exotic plants can sometimes flourish in different environments.

While she never mentioned peonies in the same breath as her other collections, Elsie's peonies offer evidence of her growing horticultural sophistication. She imported roots

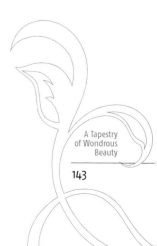

On occasion Robert Wilson Reford did photographic studies of the plants at Estevan, such as these peonies on The Long Walk.

from two of the great peony growers in England – Kelways and Barr & Sons. In 1931, her order book shows that she took delivery of 842 peonies, spending more than $600 on the purchase. This was gardening on a grand scale.

The poetic names of the peonies in her collection, 'Monsieur Jules Elie,' 'Souvenir de Maxime Cornu,' 'Avant Garde,' 'Duchesse de Nemours,' 'Couronne d'Or,' 'Claire Dubois,' and 'Félix Crousse,' illustrate how many were developed in France. While peonies had been cultivated in China and Japan for centuries, generations of French breeders were active from the 1850s onwards, creating many of the peonies that Elsie Reford collected and loved. Peonies were popular because they were ideal both in the garden and as cut flowers. Elsie Reford planted many of hers on The Long Walk, where their form and mass provide a verdant backdrop to the other plantings. Their stems burst forth soon after the snow melts and their ample foliage gives way to full bloom in the last week of June. Elsie designed The Long Walk to be approached by ascending several steps. Arriving at the top, the mass of bloom is breathtaking. Two hundred peonies on either side of The Long Walk greet the onlooker. They remain one of her garden's signature elements. And while they appear identical when viewed from afar, on closer inspection the characteristics of the more than a dozen cultivars become manifest, their single or double flowers and distinctive foliage continuing to intrigue admiring visitors.

Elsie Reford's diaries hint at her favourite peony colours, "finest scarlet crimson," "a lovely extremely pale lemony green," "semi-double magnificent bright pink," "beautiful single salmon pink." She created a white peony garden, but this appears to have been supplanted by her later enthusiasm for roses. The white peonies were moved to the cutting garden, where they provided ample material for the bouquets that she and Bufton fashioned to grace the table at the entrance to Estevan Lodge.

While enchantingly beautiful, peonies brought Elsie their share of frustration. Many of the cultivars had stems that were unable to support the saucer-sized flowers. One peony historian, Jane Fearnly Whittingstall, compared the peonies bred at the turn of the century to the overblown fashions of the era, "elaborate, heavy blossoms on slender stems, reminiscent of big hairstyles and slender necks." Peonies were susceptible to the crashing summer rainstorms that could lay them low and leave their petals littering the pathways. As our gardening staff today know only too well, every summer storm means hours of sweeping The Long Walk and staking the peonies in anticipation of the next visitor and the next storm.

As Elsie Reford's interest developed and her expertise grew, she began seeking ever more exotic cultivars. The first peonies she planted, though lovely, were fairly common. In the 1930s and 1940s she began searching for ever more unusual specimens. She imported eight tree peonies from Kelways in 1933 and wild species peonies from Barr & Sons in 1936. She then began experimenting with the hybrids developed by Arthur Percy Saunders. Saunders was a Canadian-born professor of chemistry at Hamilton College in Clinton, New York, who made more than 100 crosses between the various species and produced several peonies of exquisite finesse and beauty.

Elsie Reford evolved naturally from amateur gardener to horticultural collector. Her success with then untried perennials encouraged her to try increasingly unusual plants. And as her garden began to attract the occasional visitor, she became more aware of the range of plants available. She was also anxious to display her growing prowess as a gardener.

Sometimes her success exceeded even her own expectations. The *Paeonia mlokosewitschii* is highly prized because it is the only true yellow herbaceous peony. Other collectors who

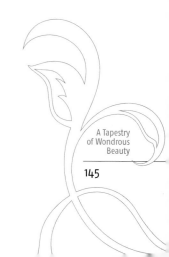

A Tapestry
of Wondrous
Beauty

145

"Magnificent, bright pink," was how
Elsie Reford described the colour
of some of her favourite peonies.

manage to cultivate this peony and make it bloom, mourn its fleeting flowering period – as brief as four hours. Elsie Reford found that it bloomed for almost two weeks at Estevan, the cool, pure air of the Lower St. Lawrence perhaps contributing to the prolongation of its beauty. This is just one of several peonies recently reintroduced to our collection. In the past three years, with the assistance of our horticulturist, Patricia Gallant, and Mary Pratte of the Canadian Peony Society, we have begun to piece together information about Elsie Reford's peony collection and identify many of the plants in the gardens. The task is formidable and illustrates the importance of continuity in gardens and gardening. When Elsie Reford left the gardens and Wyndham Coffin retired in 1964, much of the knowledge went with them. In the 1960s and 1970s, experts like Henry Teuscher and Normand Corneillier of the Montreal Botanical Garden spent hours to make an inventory of the plants that Elsie Reford had collected and planted years earlier. The seemingly insurmountable task of identifying her garden plants has required careful study and the assistance of botanists and taxonomists. Even today, hundreds remain to be precisely identified.

Elsie Reford's other collections were also ground-breaking. For instance, she is credited with introducing azaleas to Quebec gardens. Gathering specimens from several locations in England, she revelled in their lush colours. Their bright, clashing sorbet tones of bloom in mid-June continue to provide a riotous contrast with the soft greens of the ferns and spruce trees in the surrounding forest. Entirely exotic, nevertheless the azaleas do not seem out of place. Their brief appearance marks the beginning of the high flowering season that continues through the end of August.

Sometimes her zeal for collecting plants led to uncharted territory. Her love of the distinctive blue colour of the bloom of gentians inspired her to create what was a unique display of these diminutive alpine plants. Native to mountainous regions the world over,

The Gentian Garden was one of Elsie Reford's last horticultural projects. These slight, entrancing flowers inspired her to create long curving beds to display their intense blue beauty.

Gentiana septemfida.

Gentiana sino-ornata.

gentians produce flowers of stunning intensity. "A turquoise blue at its very finest... the incomparable glorious flower of the *Wellsii* hybrid in its outmost brilliancy of blue," was how she described her favourite, the *Gentiana* x *macaulayi* 'Wells's Variety' (syn. *G.* 'Welsii'). Her other preferred gentian was the *Gentiana farreri*. Her search for this elusive plant was doubtless inspired by plant explorer Reginald Farrer's description: "In no other plant... do I know such a shattering acuteness of colour; it is like a clear sky soon after sunrise, shrill and translucent, as if it had a light inside. It literally burns in the alpine turf like an electric jewel, an incandescent turquoise." Novelist and garden writer Vita Sackville-West approvingly cited Farrer's description of the gentian as an example of the best garden prose ever written. But like others, she found the plant demanding and occasionally exasperating.

Elsie Reford took pride in developing one of the few gentian gardens in the world: "There is a certain quality about these entrancing flowers, something that is perhaps best described as an aloofness in character which renders their combination with other plants not only difficult but which is apt to produce an effect of a sin committed against horticultural good taste." She thus created two long curved beds to display them adjacent to her growing collection of alpine plants, but not too close to contrast with their softer colours. Emerging discreetly into bloom in September, they complete the garden's floral tableau, disappearing beneath the first snows in late October or early November.

Her passion for gentians illustrates how much time Elsie Reford was dedicating to Estevan. Her wish to stay on later and later in the season led her to seek out plants that would bloom through the last days of summer. The scale of her plantings is impressive. In 1944, she wrote, "into the borders of the Gentian Walk there were replanted in October three thousand three hundred and fifty four *G.* 'Welsii', many were sent to other

Solomon's seal *(Polygonatum multiflorum)*.

Purple loosestrife *(lythrum salicaria)* is thought to be a noxious weed, but like other plants has its own beauty.

Rodgersia *(Rodgersia podophylla)*.

gardens while over two thousand were put into reserve to await the day when more time and labour will become available for the pursuit of the ancient craft of gardening – when the heavy war clouds will cease to cast their long, dark shadows of sorrow and peace will return to men's lives over the face of the earth."

She was also a plant thief. What she did not grow, she occasionally dug up. In her diaries she frequently records driving through the countryside in search of plants for her gardens. She was fortunate in owning stretches of the Mitis River and would sometimes hike to the water's edge to collect plants. She would also dig up specimens from ditches and fields in the backcountry. In 1931, she mentions planting 300 ferns throughout the gardens, most of them collected from the woods and farms nearby. Sometimes she would go further afield, driving as far as the Matane River, 30 miles east of her gardens, in search of tall ferns to add to her beds in the autumn.

The plant collections at Grand-Metis were not limited to flowers, of course. Estevan was a self-contained estate that lived off the produce grown on the site and on the farms that formed part of the domain. Robert Wilson Reford was particularly involved in the running of the farms and surveying the crops. When foodstuffs grew scarce during the Second World War, he began experimenting with various crops, particularly safflower and sunflowers. He became convinced that sunflowers had a future in offering an alternative to the vegetable oils commonly used for cooking. He prepared trial fields, and sent the sunflower seeds and oil to the Department of Agriculture in Ottawa for analysis. He also transformed the crop into meal for pigs, feed for chickens and seed for birds.

Even when away from her gardens, Elsie thought often of them. And like many of us, the arrival of the seed catalogues was a highlight of the garden year. She wrote to my

A Tapestry
of Wondrous
Beauty

Kentucky bluegrass
in the Meadow Garden.

"...it is something far lovelier than that; it is a turquoise blue at its very finest and it is the crossing of this shade with the intensively rich royal blue of G. sino-ornata that has given us the incomparable glorious flower of the Wellsii hybrid in its outmost brilliancy of blue..."

Elsie Reford, *Gentians at Estevan Lodge*

Common foxglove *(Digitalis purpurea)*.

father in January 1956, "now that the seed catalogues are coming in I begin to feel so much nearer the summer and the garden. I never yet have learned not to be carried away by the catalogues nor do I cease, after all these years, to make lists which have to be cut and cut again down to more reasonable proportions." She was not always able to contain herself. Her sense of proportion was exaggerated, even by today's standards. She would often order dozens, even hundreds of plants, overcome by enthusiasm and eager to try new varieties or expand to hitherto unplanted parts of the gardens. Even as her body weakened and her ability to garden diminished, her horticultural curiosity was undimmed. Well into her 80s and up to her last summer spent at the gardens in 1958, she was still planning new beds and preparing for the arrival of new plants.

Elsie Reford had a fertile mind. Because she was essentially self-taught and relied on advice culled from books and other gardeners, she was astute about planning and preparing her garden. Little was left to improvisation. When she began to develop new gardens, she did so with rigour. Her interest in plant collections also led her to create particular habitats for particular plants. And so each species was provided with a specially prepared home. The right drainage, the right sun exposure, the right soil, were all essential ingredients to her success.

My great-grandmother took a hands-on attitude. She was not an armchair director with a host of gardeners doing her bidding. There are hundreds of photographs of her kneeling in one bed or another, pulling out weeds or nurturing her specimens. Sometimes her gardening brought her to the point of exhaustion. "I am sorry to write you a birthday letter by means of the typing machine instead of with my pen," she confessed to my father in 1943, "but after using the trowel all morning somehow or other the overexertion of one set of muscles seems to paralyse others..." Nor did she believe in elabo-

Elsie taking a reading from her sundial.

Wood anemone
(*Anemone nemorosa* cv.).

Roses in bloom.

rate tools or facilities. She sometimes began plants in her Drummond Street home in Montreal. Later, she built a small greenhouse at Estevan where Wyndham Coffin would start plants in the spring for transplanting in May or June after she arrived.

The job and joy of gardening is one of making constant improvements. And Elsie's garden was in perpetual motion. Spring, summer or fall, she wandered her garden, often pen in hand, noting improvements, listing plants to be moved, and chronicling her successes and failures. Trial and error, she wrote, were her constant companions. And this process was one that she found both tantalizing and exciting. "Made a thorough inspection of all gardens," she wrote on May 25, 1941, "and took notes for future improvements." Every year she would arrive in late May and reconnoitre her domain. Things did not always go her way. Like other gardeners, she fretted during the winter months, anxious about how her gardens would survive the cold temperatures. She was often pleasantly surprised. At the end of her first day in the gardens in May 1940, she wrote, "spent the day in a fairly thorough inspection of gardens – and first of all of peonies imported from Barr late last autumn – so late that the chances were against them surviving. Every single one has survived and all are coming up well."

But on occasion nature wrought its effects. "The terrible disaster along the brook which rose over five feet and did terrible damage in consequence is a fearful thing to cope with at any season but this year with so little labour it is a heart break. Wyndham and one other man are labouring hard from 6 a.m. to make good the raw edges along Boris' garden from where we have lost about 50 of my finest lilies..." Today, we place wooden palisades in the brook to ensure that the rushing water follows its timeworn path through the gardens and does not overflow its banks – continuing a method adopted by Elsie Reford's gardeners in the 1950s.

The garden is remarkably free of ornamentation, save for the occasional birdbath and bench.

One of the last photographs of Elsie Reford in her gardens, shortly before her final departure from Estevan in 1958.

Only on occasion were the gardens opened to visitors. Elsie did so on August 2, 1941 in aid of the Queen's Fund for Air Raid victims. She sometimes received distinguished visitors who had read her articles or somehow heard of her unique garden. Henry Teuscher, the conservator of the Montreal Botanical Garden, wrote of her achievements in glowing terms:

"With these conditions, partly natural and partly created, to start with, the owner proceeded to systematically ameliorate the rather heavy, acid clay soil of very low fertility through the incorporation of large amounts of humus and compost. This took several years of untiring effort, and in the meantime experiments were started with the establishment of suitable plants. The final result is a large rambling garden of almost unbelievable richness. Asiatic Gentians, especially the hybrid *G.* x *macaulayi* 'Wells's Variety' but also *G. farreri* and *G. sino-ornata* which are the despair of gardeners in milder climates, form extensive lawns with uncountable thousands of blossoms. The European *G. acaulis* behaves in a similar manner. Azaleas and Rhododendrons, including several rare Asiatic species, act as if they were at home. Primulas of many species run riot. Lilies, of which the garden contains a fine collection of species and hybrids, develop in a manner I have never seen elsewhere, forming huge clumps of over man-high stalls with dozens of blossoms. Their preference for a shading of the lower part of the plant has been cleverly considered, and in consequence they have usually been established between peonies or low shrubs, etc. Miss Preston, the eminent Ottawa horticulturist, who visited the place, could not get over her amazement when she saw her own lily hybrids in a state of vigour and beauty which she did not know they could attain. Himalayan blue poppies (*Betonicifolia*) – with which by the way we do not succeed at Montreal – are established at the edge of a spruce grove, where they attain a height of over six feet and occasionally even seed themselves. Even Peruvian lilies (*Alstroemeria aurea*), which are generally considered to be tender

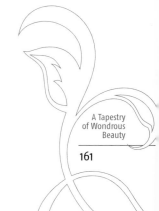

A Tapestry
of Wondrous
Beauty

161

"Lilies have been planted, but with due regard to their aversion to being crowded, in shrub gardens, with perennials, with floribunda and polyantha roses, in pockets of rock gardens and in fact anywhere considered worthy of their unequalled loveliness."

Elsie Reford, *A Lily Garden in the Lower St. Lawrence Valley*

The Japanese primrose
(*Primula japonica*).

north of hardiness zone 5, survive outdoors under the ample blanket of snow and increase to such an extent that they actually become weedy. To see this garden at the end of June is an unforgettable experience, because the late spring and the short summer season cause plants to flower together which elsewhere are months apart, and the wealth of bloom is simply overwhelming."

Elsie Reford laid no claim to being a plantsman or an expert gardener. As both collector and gardener, she did show considerable talent. Her choice of plants was inspired by the gardeners and garden writers of the day. But her adventurous spirit led her to try plants that no one had ever attempted to grow before. Her reward was the "tapestry of wondrous beauty...woven from flowers gay, brilliant and proud, timid and delicate and sweet."

Farmer's field, St. Octave-de-Métis.

Pages 166–167: "Sous la pelouse, le jardin"
from the 2nd edition of the International Garden
Festival, 2001, Sophie Beaudoin, Marie-Ève Cardinal,
Marie Gauthier (Groupe Cardinal Hardy).

"Paddling out these evenings into the sunset is like entering the porch of Heaven. Nothing could be more wonderfully beautiful or speak more of divine promise."

Elsie Reford, September 10, 1911

Epilogue

The Porch of Heaven

Closing the door of her home at the top of Drummond Street and making her way down the hill to the railway station for the trip to Metis was a familiar ritual to Elsie Reford. The road to paradise was one she had travelled for more than 50 years.

At some point during the summer of 1958, Elsie decided it would be her last at Estevan. When she left Grand-Metis in October 1958, she realized that the book on her garden had closed and that her own life was nearing its end. Restrained and emotionally contained, only rarely can one detect in her letters any hint of sadness at being unable to return to her beloved gardens. That her affection for Estevan continued is evident from her letters. She even asked Bufton, her faithful butler of almost 50 years, to venture into the gardens and take snapshots for her. He continued this horticultural espionage for several years, nourishing her need to keep track of the gardens' progress as well as the successes and failures of her favourite plants.

Leaving Metis for the last time must have been a wrenching experience. Elsie doubtless took solace in the fact that her oldest son shared her love of the region and its people. Bruce Reford was a career soldier who had a distinguished record of military service with the Irish Guards from 1914 through 1946, serving in England, Ireland, Scotland, Belgium, France, Egypt and Palestine. He retired with the rank of Brigadier and returned to Canada in 1946. After living for several years on Vancouver Island, he moved to Quebec in 1954 after his mother made him a gift of Estevan. He had grown up there and learned to ride, shoot and fish along the banks of the Mitis River. He loved the countryside and relished the simple pleasures of country life. He knew the locals better than they knew him, able to trace their genealogy and regale them with stories from his past and theirs. A giant of a man, he possessed both charm and a common touch. In returning to Estevan, Bruce Reford had come home.

He moved to Grand-Metis in 1955 and winterized parts of the house so that he could live there year round. But he also began to consider what, for his mother, would have been unimaginable – the sale of Estevan Lodge and the gardens. Bruce Reford's second wife, Elspet, was an avid gardener and enjoyed puttering in the beds created by her mother-in-law. But she was also a pragmatic woman and realized that her husband lacked the means to maintain the gardens and property his mother had given him. And the difficulty of finding an abundant source of potable water bedevilled them. Despite repeated efforts, every drill-hole proved useless because saltwater from the St. Lawrence polluted the wells and made the water undrinkable. By 1960, he was getting desperate: "having had to spend a great deal on it already, I cannot afford to keep up the garden any longer, and if nothing can be done the weeds will take over." Bruce Reford sought a buyer for Estevan.

With the help of Henry Teuscher, who had admired the gardens since his first visit in 1941, Bruce Reford's offer elicited an enthusiastic response in the corridors of power. His decision to sell Estevan happened to coincide with a major shift in government policy. The Quebec authorities were beginning to take an interest in tourism development and sought an active role in developing new sites and attractions. In September 1961, the government of Jean Lesage announced the purchase of the gardens. Bruce Reford was paid $85,000 for Estevan Lodge, the outbuildings, gardens and more than 80 acres of property on both sides of the Mitis River. The news was greeted with enthusiasm. The headline in the local newspaper heralded the future of the gardens and the region, "*Grand-Métis: premier poste touristique du grand réseau gaspésien.*"

When she got wind of her son's plans, Elsie Reford was lukewarm. But as news of the purchase and the government's scheme for the preservation of the gardens became clearer, she expressed reserved enthusiasm. "The government has announced that the garden is to be kept up as formerly and the house to serve in time as a museum," she wrote to my father. "I think if these plans are adhered to, that if it was not held for the family as I intended it should be, it all seems better than I had believed would be possible."

The transition from private to public garden is never easy. The garden historian can find the vestiges of several dozen important gardens in Quebec that have disappeared through neglect or development. Elsie Reford's gardens are one of the happy exceptions to this rule. They survived the owner's departure and made a successful transition to the public arena.

The gardens were opened to visitors for the first time on June 24, 1962. Admission price to "Le Domaine Reford" was set at 25 cents per adult; children were let in free when accompanied by an adult. Success was immediate. "During the summer, we received a great many visitors at Métis," wrote Richard Côté of the department of tourism to Henry Teuscher, "on some days, there were a thousand persons walking around the paths of the garden, and all this without there having been any official publicity or signs on the highway."

The popularity of the gardens has grown ever since, reaching 100,000 visitors annually by the 1990s. Successive managers established the principles ensuring that the alterations made to Elsie Reford's gardens were minor and respectful of their creator. The paths were widened to accommodate the public but the size and configuration of the beds were left intact. Rather than undertake a wholesale transformation, successive directors, David Gendron, Robert Castonguay and Fernand Lavoie, implemented the custodial principles of maintaining the gardens in Elsie's spirit. The organization that offered services in Estevan Lodge – the Ateliers Plein Soleil, led by Père André Boutin and Thérèse Beaulieu-Roy – worked to preserve the fabric of the building and created a museum to explain the history of the gardens and of the region. The gardens were opened under the name "Le Domaine Reford," later called "Parc Métis," and have been known as "Les Jardins de Métis" since the 1980s.

In June 1994, the Quebec government announced its intention to privatize the gardens and seek a local organization to take on their ownership and development. Within weeks, the Ateliers Plein Soleil and several members of the Reford family submitted their joint proposal to acquire the gardens. The bid was ultimately successful and the sale completed in July 1995. The gardens are now owned by Les Amis des Jardins de Métis, a non-profit organization and registered charity dedicated to maintaining the gardens and keeping them open to the public. The organization has undertaken improvements to the gardens, the restoration of Estevan Lodge, the construction of a new visitor centre and the conservation of ecosytems along the Mitis River and the St. Lawrence. Les Amis also initiated the International Garden Festival, which debuted in 2000 and is widely recognized as one of the foremost contemporary garden design events in the world. The success story of the gardens has become the pride of an entire region. As it has for more than a century, the property provides employment for local residents. As many as 100 people work on the site during the high season. With the help of members, donors, government partners, sponsors, foundations and friends, the gardens

The Reford
Gardens

have grown into one of the leading tourist attractions in eastern Canada and one of the most dynamic cultural organizations in Quebec.

People sometimes ask me what I think my great-grandmother would have thought of the transformation and of the visitors who flock to see the gardens every summer. It is certain that Elsie Reford never envisioned Estevan as a public attraction. But she was immensely proud of her gardens and enjoyed sharing them with visitors. Remembering her horror at the first motor car that rolled up to Metis in 1912, she would doubtless find the vehicles, the dust and the din incompatible with the stillness of her perfect world. She would also be surprised by her gardens' popularity today. But the sight of visitors meandering in quiet rapture along the pathways she designed and built, notebook in hand, writing down the names of the plants she had selected and planted years earlier, would have pleased her. Elsie's very private paradise is now a public one. And her adventure in gardening is today shared with thousands of visitors every summer.

William Stephen and Elspet Smith and their family emigrated to Canada from Scotland between 1847 and 1850.

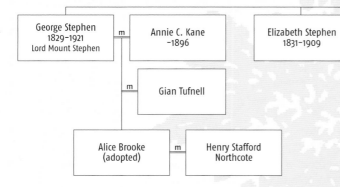

| William Stephen 1801–1891 | m | Elspet Smith 1804–1892 |

| George Stephen 1829–1921 Lord Mount Stephen | m | Annie C. Kane –1896 | | Elizabeth Stephen 1831–1909 | James Stephen 1833–1895 | Eleonora Stephen 1835–1916 |

m — Gian Tufnell

Alice Brooke (adopted) — m — Henry Stafford Northcote

Lord Mount Stephen (seated) with Elsie Reford's parents, Robert and Elsie Meighen.

Bruce Reford and his first wife, Evelyn Margaret Robinson MacInnes.

Elsie and her family, bound for England, on board the Cunard liner, RMS *Ausonia*.

Michael and Robert William Reford beside Page's Brook, circa 1930.

Family Tree

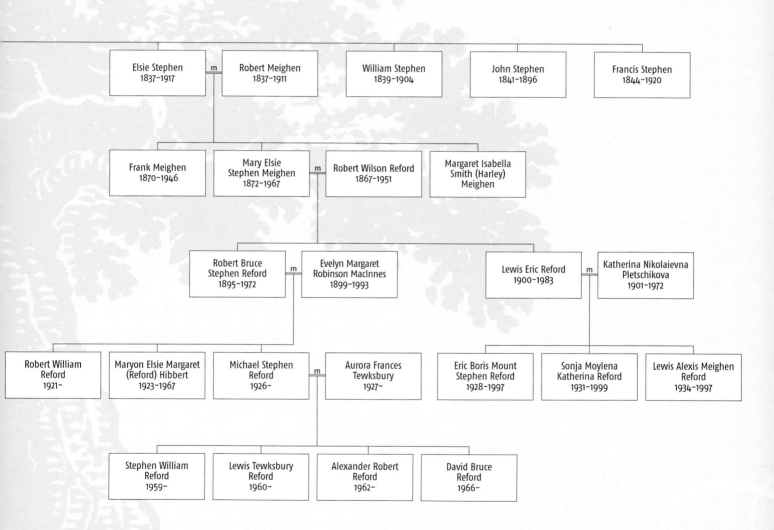

| Elsie Stephen 1837–1917 | m | Robert Meighen 1837–1911 | | William Stephen 1839–1904 | | John Stephen 1841–1896 | | Francis Stephen 1844–1920 |

Frank Meighen 1870–1946

Mary Elsie Stephen Meighen 1872–1967 — m — Robert Wilson Reford 1867–1951

Margaret Isabella Smith (Harley) Meighen

Robert Bruce Stephen Reford 1895–1972 — m — Evelyn Margaret Robinson MacInnes 1899–1993

Lewis Eric Reford 1900–1983 — m — Katherina Nikolaievna Pletschikova 1901–1972

Robert William Reford 1921–

Maryon Elsie Margaret (Reford) Hibbert 1923–1967

Michael Stephen Reford 1926– — m — Aurora Frances Tewksbury 1927–

Eric Boris Mount Stephen Reford 1928–1997

Sonja Moylena Katherina Reford 1931–1999

Lewis Alexis Meighen Reford 1934–1997

Stephen William Reford 1959–

Lewis Tewksbury Reford 1960–

Alexander Robert Reford 1962–

David Bruce Reford 1966–

Photographic Credits

Further Information
To find out more about the gardens, you can visit the Jardins de Métis / Reford Gardens website, www.jardinsmetis.com or www.refordgardens.com

You can also reach the gardens at the following address:
Jardins de Métis / Reford Gardens
200 route 132
Grand-Métis (Québec) Canada GoJ 1Zo
(418) 775-2222
jardins@jardinsmetis.com
reford@refordgardens.com

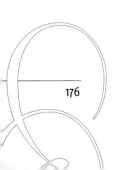

Elsie Reford kept a meticulous daily diary about her work in the gardens. She submitted two articles on her lily collection to horticultural journals, which were published in 1939 and 1949 respectively. A third article, on her collection of gentians, was not published in her lifetime, but was included in a collection of garden writing in Canada published in 1995.

ALEXANDER, COLONEL SIR JAMES EDWARD, *Salmon Fishing in Canada*. London: Green, Longman, and Roberts, 1860.

BEAULIEU-ROY, THÉRÈSE, *Métis, lieu de rencontre et de floraison*. Les Ateliers Plein Soleil, 2002.

BOUCHETTE, JOSEPH, *Topographical Dictionary of Lower Canada*. London: Faden William, 1815.

Chambres Vertes. Festival international de jardins Jardins de Métis. Première édition, Été 2000 / *Garden Rooms*. International Garden Festival / Reford Gardens, First Edition, Summer 2000. Montreal: Musée d'art contemporain de Montréal, 2001.

Chambres Vertes. Festival international de jardins Jardins de Métis. Deuxième édition / *Garden Rooms*. International Garden Festival, Jardins de Métis. Montreal: Les 400 Coups, 2002.

GILBERT, HEATHER, *Awakening Continent. The Life of Lord Mount Stephen*. Aberdeen University Press, 1965.

GILBERT, HEATHER, *The End of the Road. The Life of Lord Mount Stephen*. Aberdeen University Press, 1977.

NATIONAL GALLERY OF SCOTLAND, "Leonardo da Vinci—The Mystery of the *Madonna of the Yarnwinder*," Martin Kemp, ed., Edinburgh : The Trustees of the National Galleries of Scotland, 1992, p. 41.

REFORD, ALEXANDER, Biographies of George Stephen (Volume XV), Robert Reford (Volume XIV), Robert Meighen (Volume XIV) and Donald Smith (Volume XIV), *Dictionary of Canadian Biography*. The DCB is available on line at www.biographi.ca

REFORD, ALEXANDER, *Reford Gardens*. Montreal: Fides, 2001.

REFORD, ALEXANDER, "Les Jardins d'Elsie Reford," *Estuaire*, June 2002 (article available on the Reford Gardens' website).

REFORD, ALEXANDER, "The Gardens of Elsie Reford," *Journal of the New England Garden History Society*, Volume 9, Fall 2001 (article available on the Reford Gardens' website).

REFORD, ELSIE, "Lilies at Estevan Lodge, Grand-Metis, Province of Quebec, Canada." *The Royal Horticultural Society Lily Yearbook*, Number 8, 1939, p. 7-14.

REFORD, ELSIE, "A Lily Garden in the Lower St. Lawrence Valley." *The Lily Yearbook of the North American Lily Society*, Number 2, 1949, p. 70-75.

REFORD, ELSIE, *Gentians at Estevan Lodge*. Unpublished typescript.

REFORD, ELSIE, "*Gentiana macaulayi* variety *welsii* at Estevan Lodge, Grand-Metis, P.Q. Canada," published in *Garden Voices, Two Centuries of Canadian Garden Writing*, Edwinna Von Baeyer and Pleasance Crawford, eds., Toronto: Random House, 1995, p. 238-242.

REFORD, ROBERT WILLIAM, *Metis Memories*, to be published in 2004.

Table of Contents

Printed in Canada at
Interglobe Printing Inc.
in May 2004.